Both Feet Firmly Planted in Midair

JOHN McNEILL
Both Feet Firmly Planted in Midair

My Spiritual Journey

Westminster John Knox Press
Louisville, Kentucky

Scripture quotations, unless otherwise noted, are from the New Revised Standard Version of the Bible copyright © 1989 by the Division of Christian Education of the National Council of the Churches of Christ in the U.S.A. and are used by permission.

Grateful acknowledgment is made to the following for permission to reprint copyrighted material: Daniel Berrigan, S.J., *Portraits of Those Whom I Love* (New York: Crossroad, 1982). Delacorte Press/ Seymour Lawerence, a division of Bantam Doubleday Dell Publishing Group, Inc., from *Slaughterhouse-Five* by Kurt Vonnegut, Jr. Copyright © 1968, 1969 by Kurt Vonnegut, Jr. Used by permission. Mary Hunt, "John McNeill: The Long View Is Short," *National Catholic Reporter*, May 12, 1996. Warner Brothers Publications U.S. Inc., Miami, FL 33014, "Taking a Chance on Love," by Vernon Duke, John Latouche, and Ted Fetter © 1940 (Renewed) EMI Miller Catalog Inc. All rights reserved. Used by permission.

Book and cover design by Jennifer K. Cox
Cover photograph New York Daily News

First edition
Published by Westminster John Knox Press
Louisville, Kentucky

This book is printed on acid-free paper that meets the American National Standards Institute Z39.48 standard. ♾

PRINTED IN THE UNITED STATES OF AMERICA
98 99 00 01 02 03 04 05 06 07 — 10 9 8 7 6 5 4 3 2 1

Library of Congress Cataloging-in-Publication Data
McNeill, John, 1925–
    Both feet firmly planted in midair : my spiritual journey / John McNeill. — 1st. ed.
      p.   cm.
    Includes bibliographical references.
    ISBN 0-664-25808-5 (alk. paper)
    1. McNeill, John, 1925– .   2. Jesuits—United States—Biography.
3. Ex-priests, Catholic—United States—Biography.   4. Gay clergy—United States—Biography.
5. Catholic gays—United States—Biography.   I. Title.
BX4668.3.M38A3   1998
271'.5302—dc21   98–15197
[B]

Our God dwells within us and
the only way we can become
one with our God is to become
one with our authentic self.

Maurice Blondel, *Principle of Immanence*

⌒

Help us to embrace the world you have given us,
and transform the darkness of its pain
into the life and joy of Easter.

Papal Opening Prayer: Fifth Sunday in Lent, 1979

Contents

Preface

In September of 1979, Pope John Paul II summoned all the Jesuit leaders in Rome—the General, Pedro Arrupé; his assistant, Vincent O'Keefe; all the regional assistants representing the various provinces all over the world—thirty in all. The pope expressed extreme dissatisfaction with the Jesuit order, declaring he was "upset with the general lowering of sexual standards in religious life, including homosexuality, a lack of loyalty to the Vatican and central authorities."

The pontiff stated he was also worried by Jesuit theologians speaking out against traditional doctrine and by those actively espousing leftist social policies in various parts of the world. "I urge you . . . to bring remedy with due firmness to these deplored deficiencies," the pope demanded of the Jesuit leaders. To make his point, he discussed individual cases in detail. One example was the Reverend John McNeill, whose 1976 book, *The Church and the Homosexual*, sharply attacked the church's official teaching on homosexuality. What might have called the pope's attention to me and my book was the fact that it had just been published in Italian by Mondadori of Milan. The other Jesuit the pope mentioned by name was the Reverend Fernando Cardenal of Nicaragua, who had played a key role in the overthrow of the regime of General Anastasio Somoza earlier that year and taken a role in the Sandinista government.

I think it was providential that I did not learn until many years later that the pope denounced both me and my book by name at that meeting. At that early stage of my ministry, I would have been devastated to feel even partly personally responsible for the falling out between the Jesuits and the papacy. Eventually, the pope deposed Pedro Arrupé as General and appointed in his place an "inquisitor" to head the Jesuits. He also replaced the Jesuits with Opus Dei as his most trusted advisors.

Shortly after that meeting, Fernando Cardenal was ordered to leave his official post with the Sandinista government or be expelled from the Jesuits. As for me, I was ordered by the Vatican to silence in the public media on the issue of homosexuality and sexual ethics. I was able to obey that order for the next nine years.

These memoirs describe the important events on my spiritual journey that led to that meeting of the pope with the Jesuit leaders in Rome. My consequent expulsion from the Jesuits opened the door to what I now see as my real priesthood and ministry to my lesbian sisters and gay brothers and helped me to exercise that ministry on a much more universal and ecumenical level.

From 1955 to 1959, I pursued a four-year course in theology at Woodstock Seminary. One of my favorite teachers there was Gustave Weigle, a brilliant and passionate man, very active in Protestant-Catholic ecumenical dialogue. During the Second Vatican Council, he served as liaison in Rome for non-Catholic observers.

I had read an account of a dialogue Gustave held with Martin Buber. It struck me that something he was reported to have said in that dialogue contradicted a position he held in his lectures at Woodstock. With youthful fervor, I got up my courage and went to his office. I confronted him with what I perceived as the contradiction and asked, "Would the real Gustave Weigle please stand up!" There was an ominous silence as Gustave's face became purple with rage. I backed quickly to the door and made my exit before he could explode.

A few weeks later, the faculty met to discuss the qualifications of the fourth-year theologians who were about to graduate from Woodstock. Recommendations had to be made to the New York and Maryland provincials as to what ministry in the Society of Jesus the graduates would be best suited. I am told that when my name came up and Gustave Weigle was asked to give his opinion, he asserted in his German accent, "John McNeill is the only Jesuit I know who has *both feet firmly planted in midair*. Wherever he goes, whatever he does, there will be trouble, trouble, trouble!"

Gustave died a few years after the Council. As it turned out, his warning about me was quite prophetic.

Acknowledgments

I wish to acknowledge with gratitude all the people who helped me by reading the manuscript of this autobiography, making suggestions for its development, and encouraging me to persevere in writing this demanding and difficult book.

First of all, I am grateful to Margaret and Larry Kornfeld, who read the manuscript as it was in progress and made excellent suggestions on how best to tell my story. Thanks also go to Jack and Judy McMahon of the Inn at Starlight Lake, Pennsylvania, for their careful reading and editorial advice.

Finally, and most important, I wish to acknowledge all the help and encouragement and all the hours, days, weeks, and even years of work put in by my life-partner, Charles Chiarelli, without whose assistance this book would probably never have seen the light of day. His total support and patience over the two years it took to recollect and produce these memoirs made the task of writing it possible and enjoyable. Having shared my life with all its joys, sorrows, and adventures over the past thirty-two years, he was able to help me remember many details accurately; his help was indispensable.

Anyone who wishes to comment or ask questions can reach me at my e-mail address, jjmcneill@aol.com.

1

Why Buffalo?

Our home at 166 Winslow Avenue in Buffalo, New York, resembled the *All in the Family* TV home of Archie and Edith Bunker in Queens, New York. I was born in Buffalo on September 2, 1925, and had a very happy but uneventful infancy surrounded by the love of my mother and father, Mary and Charles. The first vivid, conscious memory that emerges out of that tranquil period was a sunny winter morning in 1929, when I was four years old. I was in my crib in my father's bedroom on the second floor when I became aware of a commotion in the hallway. An ambulance emergency crew was carrying my mother down the stairs in a stretcher. She cried out in pain and anguish, "What's going to happen to my babies?"

This fearful memory is the first and only one I have of my mother. I never saw her or heard her speak again. Of the five children—four brothers, Charles, Tom, Francis, and me, and one sister, Marion—I was the youngest. Fran was one year older than I, and Sis two years older. Tom was ten, and Chuck, the oldest at twelve, had a very close bond with our mother. Every day that she was in Sisters' Hospital on Main Street, he skipped lunch, ran the two miles from school to the hospital, visited with her, and then ran back to school.

One morning, my mother's sister, my Aunt Katie, burst into my bedroom and, flinging open the window, called anxiously and tearfully to the woman next door to call my father home from work. My mother had died that morning in Sisters' Hospital.

Some time later, my father came into the room and changed out of his work clothes. Watching from my crib, I saw him pausing in confusion and bursting into tears. I wanted to reach out and console him but was too terrified to speak. My father didn't speak to me and seemed totally unaware of my presence. I realized consequently that not only had I lost my mother on that twenty-third of December but also somehow I had lost the close bond I had had with my father.

My family held an old-fashioned Irish wake. My mother's open coffin was placed in the corner of the living room, where the Christmas tree would ordinarily have stood. The Christmas wreath on the front door was replaced by a black funeral wreath. With the death of my mother, my trust in the world was badly damaged. On Christmas Day, during the wake, I was sent out to play on the front porch. Aware of all the grief inside the house, my father's unavailability, and the threat of our family breaking up and all of us children being sent to an orphanage, I watched a cat stalk its prey. At that moment, I suddenly felt the whole universe, including God, was hostile. I ran in terror back into the house. All our Irish relatives were gathered to express their condolences. They were looking at me with pity and compassion that so young a child had lost his mother, but I remember interpreting their sympathy as looks of accusation. I concluded that God had taken my mother from me because I was a bad child; God was punishing me for my wickedness. I remember especially the look of pity on the face of my Great-Aunt Shawl Graham, in her nineties, whom I called "the lady with all the wrinkles in her face."

In the town of Nedrow, New York, Graham Road was named after her. We visited her on her dairy farm in the summers, and I always looked forward to sitting out on the back stoop at night to watch for falling stars. Down the road was the farm where my father was born, and we frequently stayed with my Aunt Lizzie and Uncle Frank, who lived out their lives on that farm. We sometimes stayed with my Aunt Gertrude and Uncle Leonard, who had a home in Nedrow. Those memories of visits to my father's family in Nedrow are some of the happiest of my childhood. Whenever life in Buffalo became intolerable, I entertained the illusion that was I moving in with my Uncle Frank, for whom I had a deep affection.

From my mother's wake on, I related to God primarily as a god of fear. A god who would punish a bad four-year-old by killing his mother was more like a Christian Baal than the loving father revealed by Jesus. Scripture tells us that "perfect love casts out fear" (1 John 4:18). It is equally true that perfect fear casts out all love. On that day, I began what was to become a lifetime journey, during which my relationship to God would be transformed from one of fear to one of love.

I always had a deep affection for my father, Charles. The farm in Nedrow where he was born was previously part of the Onondaga reservation, and Native American children were Dad's playmates as he grew up. Dad was one of twelve children and worked hard on the farm. He was able to attend the local one-room school for only a few years. His aunt was his teacher. Frequently, he was so tired from early morning work on the farm that he fell asleep in class and his aunt wrapped him in her shawl. But Dad was naturally very bright and learned quickly. Many years later, after World War II, I attended engineering classes with him at Burgardt High School, where he earned the credits he needed to receive a stationary engineer's license.

One of Dad's first jobs was on the Erie Barge Canal, helping to build the waterway that runs from Albany to Buffalo. While working near the town of Lyons, New York, he met my mother, Mary, at an Irish dance, and it was love at first sight. They soon married and settled in Buffalo, where Dad's job on the canal came to an end. He then took a job helping to build the breakwater in Buffalo's harbor in Lake Erie. Shortly after, he began to work at the Kelley Island Lime and Steel Corporation, a job he held for almost fifty years. Operating a huge crane, Dad unloaded mountains of sand, coal, limestone, and iron ore from barges in the harbor. Over the years, the noise of the crane deafened him. We all had to shout at the dinner table for him to hear what we were saying.

He was proud of the skills he developed over the years. Steel companies called on him to help them take inventory. After years of operating a steam shovel, he could look at a mountain of coal, for example, figure how many shovel loads it would take to move it, and estimate the tonnage. Because he was usually accurate to within a few tons, the company saved the expense of moving the coal to measure it.

Dad was deeply involved in organizing the labor unions in Buffalo. He never talked much about it, but I found out later that he had been actively involved in some of the fierce fighting against armed groups of scabs that companies brought into Buffalo from the South to break the effort to unionize. Dad occasionally expressed some feelings of guilt for his actions but always remained proud of his part in supporting the effort to establish the unions.

I had a pet dog, a fox terrier named Pug, who was my constant playmate.

Pug saw himself as my father's watchdog. When my father arrived home promptly at five-thirty every evening, the dog rushed wildly around the yard and out into the street, yapping and growling and putting on a convincing imitation of a vicious guard dog. My father became afraid that he might attack someone and we would be sued, so he had my dog "put to sleep" at the ASPCA. That was another blow to my ability to trust the world, the love of my father, and the fairness of authority.

I was a terrible klutz and, being the youngest of five children, I was the last to develop skills and vocabulary. After the war, when I was in my twenties, my father took me out one day to the Sears parking lot to teach me how to drive. I just could not coordinate operating the clutch, shifting gears, and keeping my eyes on the road. After several close calls, he gave up in disgust and never again offered to teach me. But Dad was proud of me in his own way. Several times while I spoke publicly as a student at Canisius College, which was just a few blocks away from our home, I observed Dad sitting quietly in the back of the audience.

I didn't learn to drive until I was forty, when my lover, Charlie, had the patience to try to instruct me. Even then, Charlie gave up trying to teach me to drive a car with a manual transmission. The next car we purchased had an automatic transmission. However, learning to drive so late in life, I had problems with other automotive concepts. During one evening's driving lesson, when I had to merge onto a busy highway, Charlie urgently instructed me, "Quick! Step on it!" And I calmly asked him, "When you say step on it, do you mean the brake pedal or the accelerator?"

Dad's health began to deteriorate when he was in his fifties. His first major illness was colon cancer. He underwent a colostomy and had to wear a bag the rest of his life. He was deeply ashamed of his lack of control. Although he quickly returned to work, he cut out almost all his social life. On a trip to visit me at Bellarmine Seminary near Plattsburgh, New York, in 1956, my father had a stroke that left him paralyzed on one side. I took him home on a stretcher on a train, and he spent the rest of his life in a wheelchair.

The next Sunday after bringing Dad home to Buffalo, I went to my parish church. Because I was wearing my Roman collar, I asked the Irish pastor for permission to attend the mass in the sacristy. I noticed he seemed flustered. When he got to the reading of the Gospel for the day, he turned to the congregation and announced he had misplaced the English translation and would have to translate from the Latin. He added in a stage whisper, "And there's a Jesuit in the sacristy who will be checking every word of it!"

While I was in Europe doing my doctorate studies in philosophy, Dad's diabetes acted up. Eventually, he was hospitalized, and both his legs had to be amputated. One day at Louvain when I opened Katie's weekly letter, he had written two words at the bottom of the letter: "Come home!" This was the first time he ever wrote to me. I called home and was told that he was critical and could die at any time but again he could last for several months. Selfishly, I did not want to return home and lose out on my doctorate. I asked my family to let me know when the end was in sight so I could then return.

A few days later, I was walking with a Jesuit friend from Brazil on the grounds of the Jesuit house at Chantilly, which was originally the hunting lodge of the Rothschilds, when suddenly I was taken deathly ill. I went to my room, where I vomited and felt a crushing depression. I finally fell asleep from exhaustion. In the middle of the night, I woke to the sound of knocking on the door. It was the superior of the house, who informed me he had received a phone message from Buffalo. My father had died that afternoon—exactly at the hour when I had suddenly become ill in the garden. I've always felt sure that in some mysterious way I had shared in my father's death agony. When I awoke, all signs of my illness had disappeared. I made my way immediately to the airport in Paris and took the next plane home.

It was my privilege to celebrate my father's funeral mass with my family. At the wake, the chaplain at the hospital, Father Bill Gleason, who had been my novice master, told me that just a few days before, my father had told him that he was ready for death and felt he had accomplished what God had asked of him. He was very proud of his family: his daughter, a nun; his youngest son, a Jesuit priest; and his three other sons happily married with large families. He was ready to go in peace. I regret to this day that I had not obeyed his request to "come home!" for that last meeting.

I realize now that, throughout my life, my intense longing for intimacy with God had as a source my childhood longing for a closer relationship with my father, a longing made more intense by my gay longing for male intimacy. My father's emotional distance and his discomfort with me, because I was so different from my brothers, fed my fear that God, too, would take distance from me and dislike who I was as a gay man.

2

The Battlin' Sharkeys

What can I say about my stepmother, Katie? I had such a deeply ambivalent relationship with her, one of gratitude and love and one of anger and dislike. To this day, my attitude toward Katie flips back and forth—but usually the gratitude and love prevail. Katie was the youngest in her family. She had two brothers, my uncles Tom and John, and one sister, Mary, my mother. The family home in Ireland was a thatched cottage on an island, Lumcloon, on Lough (Lake) Gara directly across from the town of Monasteraden in the county of Roscommon. As a young girl, Katie learned to play the accordion for the local fests and dances and memorized all the tunes that had been passed down from generation to generation since the thirteen hundreds and earlier. On a trip to Ireland, I met an elderly gentleman in Monasteraden who told me that as a young man, fifty years before, he used to sit on the steps of the parish church and listen to the beauty of the music coming across the waters of the lake as Katie practiced.

Katie was full of joy and fun then, and was well liked. Fifty years after she left Ireland, her friends from Roscommon would sit for hours, recalling her pranks and jokes and laughing together. Once a month the people gathered at someone's cottage to hold a *ceili* of music and dancing. The church managed to cast a shadow of doubt and fear on the simple pleasures of Katie and her friends out of a suspicion that the dances were an occasion for sin. In fact, a Passionist preacher (from the Passionist religious order, whose members specialized in "fire and brimstone" retreats that portrayed God as a god of fear) at the church during a parish mission made the statement, "May the arm wither on the ones who play the music for the ceili." My mother suffered a hysterical paralysis of her arm for a while following that sermon, but her good sense freed her from that curse and she continued to celebrate the beauty of God with her music. The Irish church my stepmother was brought up in tried to control every aspect of life through fear.

On my first visit back to my mother's home, my cousin, Tom Corcoran, drove me into the nearest town, Ballaghaderreen, to see the parish priest for permission to say mass in Monasteraden. Tom was in such a fear of the priest that when I rang the doorbell, he ran around the back of the parish house and hid. The priest, who was upstairs in his study, made me wait alone for an hour before he came down. He was contemptuous of me, saying, "Is this all you Yanks have to do, traveling around?" When he found that I was visiting my relatives on Lumcloon, he made some condescending remark about their not being half-bad. When I emerged from the priest house, I saw my cousin, a man of fifty years, peeking around the corner of the house. I asked him why he had fled. "Well, Father," he responded, "the priest thinks that we who live on the island are bad people and is always criticizing us!"

The people on the island had a unique spirit all their own. That Sunday after church, one of my cousins, a man in his seventies, asked me, "Is it true that President Kennedy announced that he planned to send men in a space rocket to the moon?" When I answered, "Yes," he chortled and told the onlookers, "See! What I read to you was true." He explained that every Sunday after mass, the people who could not read gathered around him, and he read the newspaper to them. When he read that men were going to the moon, the people laughed at him, accusing him of making it up to try to make fools of them. "They still think the moon is made of green cheese!" He told me that years ago they laughed at him when he read that men had learned to fly. "And now," he said, "they see airplanes passing overhead every day!"

Everywhere I went, people asked me to come into their backyard and bless the chickens and donkeys and other animals. One of my cousins made me wait because he wanted to give me a gift. The gift was a dozen eggs, but we had to wait until the hen laid the twelfth egg. My first night on the island, the whole clan gathered and told ghost stories well into the night. As they prepared to retire for the night, they asked me when I would celebrate the Eucharist the next day. When I said eight o'clock, all their faces fell. I realized my faux pas and suggested that perhaps twelve noon would be better. They all brightened up.

The level of fearful superstition there was the highest I've ever experienced.

The next morning I went for a walk. I discovered a circle of trees and bushes with a narrow entrance. I walked in and saw a well in the middle. When I emerged, a whole group of people had gathered at the entrance and were obviously disturbed. They explained to me that this circle was a fairy fort, a sacred pagan grove. Years ago, a man had walked in and disappeared from the face of the earth. On another occasion, one of my relatives removed the stone from the top of the well and was carrying it down the hill to use as a new lintel for his cottage. Suddenly, balls of fire came out of the well and forced him to return the stone and put it back on the well. They were afraid I would disappear or that harm would come to me, and they would be blamed. So they begged me never to go near the fort again.

The faith of these simple people was so strong that the spiritual world was more real to them than the material world in which they lived. As Meister Eckart said: "If the only prayer you ever said in your whole life is a heartfelt thank you, that will suffice." Everyone I met in Ireland began every conversation with "Thanks be to God!" One time when I was visiting my relatives on Lumcloon, a woman bicycled out from Sligo to see a man who had been cured at Our Lady's shrine at Knock. The man was a local farmer who had broken his back in a fall five years before. For four years, his sons had carried him to Knock to seek a cure, and every year they carried him back. The fifth year, however, he walked home with his sons. My Irish cousin was amused that the woman on the bicycle had traveled all that distance to see the man. "What will the woman see," my cousin asked, "but a man working in the field? His family needed him, so Our Lady cured him. You can't see a miracle." I reflected that in such an atmosphere of childlike faith, humility, trust, and gratitude, God was free to perform miracles without disrupting anyone's life or inflating anyone's ego.

My stepmother brought that kind of faith with her to Buffalo. She passed on that faith to us as the primary gift she had to give us. It was a treasure worth infinitely more than any material goods. Katie's father and my grandfather, Tom Sharkey, could not make a living on the tiny scrap of hardscrabble land he owned in Ireland. Forced to go to Scotland and find a factory job in Glasgow to feed his family, he could spend only two weeks of summer vacation with his family. He spent that time cutting hay for the farm animals. Tom's claim to fame was that he brought some plum trees back to Lumcloon. The trees flourished and became the basis for a famous plum jelly the islanders processed.

The Sharkey family was famous in the west of Ireland for their support of Irish independence from England. They were known as the "Battlin' Sharkeys." Whenever Uncle Tom Sharkey came from Syracuse to Buffalo to visit, he opened the screen door to the kitchen, tossed his hat in, and announced, "I'm the best man in the house. If anyone wishes to dispute that, let him step outside!" My father always chuckled and invited Tom in without a fight.

Another uncle, John Sharkey, a mountain of a man, lived in a boardinghouse in Buffalo and was considered the strongest man working on the railroad. Unfortunately, he was also an uncontrolled alcoholic. But every Ash Wednesday he would sober up and come to our house to visit with a big splotch of ashes on his forehead. He had his own version of the Ash Wednesday prayer: "From ashes to ashes, from dust to dust. There's the hole and in you must."

When my grandfather Tom retired and returned home to Ireland, he saw his children leave one by one for America until only Katie was left. Katie nursed her father through his final battle with cancer. After his death, my mother, who was in ill health, asked Katie to come to Buffalo to help her deal with her growing family. Katie crossed the Atlantic as a steerage passenger in the midst of World War I. Shortly after she disembarked, the ship she came on, the *Saint Augustine*, was torpedoed in New York harbor. My mother and father met Katie on Ellis Island and brought her to Buffalo.

My aunt took a job as maid with wealthy families on the west side of Buffalo and, to her death, had bitter memories of the suspicion and contempt with which she was treated by her employers. She attended the Irish dances and fell in love with another Irish emigrant, a chauffeur for the family she worked for. A few years after her arrival, tragedy struck. Her sister—my mother—became terminally ill with a kidney ailment caused in part by the birth of her five children. I believed, because I was the last to be born, that I was the cause of my mother's illness. Katie quit her job and moved in to take care of her sister and help with us children.

Katie once told me that she was afraid of my father when she first met him and did not like him. I suspect that the feeling was mutual. But Dad had no choice but to accept Katie's help with his ailing wife and five children. After my mother's death, Katie consulted with the local priest and decided to follow an ancient Irish tradition. When a woman dies and leaves young children, it was the custom in Irish culture that her unmarried sister had the duty to marry her husband and together take a vow of chastity to live as brother and sister. Katie was aware that, unless she married my father, her sister's five children would have to be sent to an orphanage. She had promised Mary on her deathbed that she would take care of her children. Katie felt that if she had any children of her own she would favor them over her sister's children. She had seen this happen among relatives in Ireland and therefore made the decision never to have any children but raise her sister's children as if they were her own. My father, feeling he had no real options, went along with Katie's decision.

A few months after my mother's death, they went to St. Nicholas Church on Utica Street. My father received a dispensation to marry his deceased wife's sister, and they vowed to live together as brother and sister. Both of them sacrificed any hope of a personal love life for the sake of us children. Katie gave up her job and her boyfriend. I met him forty years later, and he was still in love with Katie. Dad gave up any possibility of a sexual life. We children grew up with the burden of our responsibility for our parents' frustration and unhappiness.

When Katie was in a good mood, she could be playful and humorous. She played the accordion, and I danced Irish jigs. She waited to see us rounding the corner on our way home from St. Nicholas parochial school and put on the teakettle to boil. As soon as we came in, we gathered around the kitchen table for tea and cookies, while she demanded to learn all the news of that day at school. I remember those times as filled with laughter.

But most of the time, Katie was in a bad mood, depressed and angry. I spent long hours hiding in my bedroom upstairs to get away from her rage. Coming home from school, I felt like I was living in the Thurber cartoon of a whole house possessed by an angry woman, reaching out to seize her husband as he came up the walk.

My father never interfered with Katie, even when on occasion her rage became abusive. More than once, when Katie thought we had misbehaved, she made us all pack our belongings and had my father drive us to the local Catholic home where children who committed crimes were sent by the courts. While we tearfully begged for mercy and forgiveness, Katie would dump us out of the car and ring the doorbell. Then she and my father drove off, only to come back and take us home again a few minutes later. One summer evening when I was about eight years old, I was playing with fire by lighting pieces of paper on the gas stove in the kitchen. The fire got out of control. In fear, I tossed a burning paper into the vestibule leading to the basement to conceal it and closed the door. It landed on a pile of papers. Luckily, my father was in the basement, spotted the fire early on, and called the fire department. The next day, to teach me not to play with fire, Katie held my hand over a gas jet flame on the stove for a few seconds. I realized later in therapy that in setting that fire I was acting out my unconscious anger. Katie learned well a lesson from the church in Ireland on how to control through fear and to distrust the control she could exercise through love.

My father was a very kind and compassionate man. He was famous for the fact that no one had ever seen him angry. Although we sensed that he did not agree with Katie's method of discipline, he refused to interfere. The few times he did disagree with her, Katie packed her bags, went to a friend's house, and refused to return until Dad went to her to apologize. Every morning, my father prepared our breakfast while Katie stayed in bed. He had us all kneel at the chairs in the living room while we said our prayers. Then he would take us to St. Nicholas Church for morning mass. Most evenings, we all knelt and said the rosary before going to bed. Our home was more like a monastery than a regular home, part of the reason why I was so attracted to religious life later on.

A few memories make clear how depressed I was at that time. In first grade, I was in terror of the authority of the sisters who taught me. One day I had diarrhea and desperately needed to go to the bathroom. But I was so afraid of calling attention to myself that I could not raise my hand and ask permission to go to the bathroom. Eventually, I could no longer control myself and let go in my pants. The sister searched the room and located the odor at my desk. She sent for my sister, Marion, who was two years ahead of me, and I was taken home in disgrace. This experience helped confirm my image of myself as inadequate to respond to the ordinary challenges of life, an image I have had to struggle with until this day. Only recently has it occurred to me to question why that five-year-old child was too terrified to raise his hand and ask to go to the toilet. Fear already had a pathological hold on that child's psyche.

Life for me at home was so miserable and unhappy that when I was ten I decided to commit suicide. Being a good Catholic, I knew that I could not take my life directly. So I decided to walk into traffic on Jefferson Avenue with my eyes closed. I was hit by a car and badly bruised. The experience was so painful that I decided to give up on suicide.

One year on the first day of school, I left all the books I had just purchased on the ground while I played ball. When I returned, they were gone; someone had stolen them. I could never get up the courage to tell anyone, especially Katie, that they were stolen, so I spent a whole year pretending to have the books necessary for class. At the end of the year, I received all U's for unsatisfactory. I remember being ridiculed by my older brothers for joining the U club. Again, terror and feelings of inadequacy ruled my life.

The nuns who taught me, for the most part, were kind and friendly. There were some exceptions. The nun who was my homeroom teacher in fifth grade told Katie that I was always daydreaming. Katie gave her permission to use any means she could to pull me out of my daydreams. The sister put me in the first row. While she read us a story each afternoon, every time she turned a page, she slapped me across the face.

The school bully, a much older boy who had failed to graduate three years in a row, stuck pins in my buttocks when he was behind me in line. As we marched single file one day down Utica Street to Jefferson Avenue under surveillance of the sisters, the bully forced me out of line. When we returned to school after lunch, the school principal called me to her office and rapped my knuckles with a wooden ruler for failing to follow orders. The injustice of it all singed my soul, and my ability to respect authority was again badly bruised. I gleefully fantasized that the bully was my prisoner. I had him tied to a post, and with great pleasure I was torturing him with fire. This revelation of my sadistic dark side shocked me and filled me with guilt.

My relationship with God was equally ambivalent during my childhood. As soon as I memorized the Latin responses for the mass, I became an altar boy and served the seven o'clock mass most mornings at St. Nicholas. I frequently thought that God might be calling me to the priesthood but thought that maybe that was hubris on my part. I felt too sinful and unworthy for so exalted a calling. My favorite prayer in childhood was "Lord, grant me the grace to know your will for me and the courage to be able to do it."

Katie definitely wanted one of Mary's sons to become a priest. She felt this was the highest honor the family could aspire to. She put pressure on each of my brothers to enter the seminary. Tom did enter but didn't last long. He was too interested in dating and drinking, so he was thrown out in his first year. Charles and Francis never gave it a thought. That left me. So Katie put a full-court press on me to be the family priest. I was her last chance. Among priests from Irish American backgrounds, there was always the saying that we were never sure if our vocation to the priesthood was ours or our mother's until forty-eight hours after she was put into her grave. For some of us, we will not be sure until we ourselves are put in our graves.

In high school, a recruiter for the Christian Brothers made a pitch for new candidates. I decided to enter their seminary. When I announced this decision at home, Katie realized that I was too young to go to a novitiate. She used reverse psychology and told me that was fine with her and when I was ready to leave, she would help me pack the bags. Taken aback by the lack of resistance, I changed my mind and decided not to enter religious life at that time.

My eighth-grade teacher was convinced that I did have a vocation to the priesthood and wanted me to go to Canisius High School in the hope that the Jesuits there would foster my vocation. But I failed to qualify for entrance there and went to Saint Joseph's Collegiate Institute instead.

When I entered my teens and began high school in 1938, I brought with me from my childhood some deep psychic wounds that continued to plague me the rest of my life. Foremost was a deep sense of inadequacy and lack of self-confidence. That wound received confirmation over and over again. Consequently, whatever I have accomplished was always accompanied with extraordinary feelings of anxiety. During every public speech I have ever given, every class I taught, and every television appearance or radio talk show, anxiety and feelings of inadequacy were always with me.

God heard my prayers and always gave me the grace to have the courage to do what I believed to be God's will. But, although I prayed continuously for relief, God never saw fit to lift that painful mood of anxiety that still continues.

This anxiety has played an important role in my spiritual life. Because of it, I have never been in danger of developing a strong sense of ego. Every time I accomplished some goal, aware that it was a result of God's help, I felt a strong sense of gratitude to God for making use of me.

I believe that my low sense of ego and my strong dependence on God's grace made it possible for God to accomplish many things by using me as God's instrument without any danger of my ego becoming inflated.

3

Coming of Age

As a child growing up in Buffalo, I was aware of a real difference between me and my brothers and schoolmates. Many aspects of my personality were unacceptable to my peers and to my family, including my total captivation with the beauty of classical music, especially the music of Mozart and Beethoven. It fed my spiritual life by giving me an insight into a lovable beauty of God that was unpolluted with images of guilt and fear.

I fully identified with an experience that Henry Adams recorded in his autobiography, *The Education of Henry Adams*. He recounted that his greatest educational experience happened despite himself and without his conscious collaboration—in fact, with his active resistance. While he was in Berlin as a young man studying international law, he frequented a beer garden where expatriate American students hung out. The orchestra at the garden played Beethoven continuously. Thinking it was part of the snobbish pretentiousness of his parents and the Boston upper class, Adams hated classical music. One night while he was alone making rings with his beer mug on the table out of boredom, his mind followed a theme from a Beethoven symphony through several of its variations. He found himself experiencing ecstatic joy over the beauty of the music. He spoke about the beauty and power of the music, which was able to "break down the prison bars of my mind." This, Adams claimed, was the greatest educational experience of his whole life.

Only many years later did I realize that my sensitivity to the beauty of music, a sensitivity not shared by my family or peers, was an important aspect of God's special gift to me in my gayness. My favorite name for God has always been Beauty. I was immediately struck when I first heard the opening line of

St. Augustine's passionate prayer from his *Confessions*, "Late have I loved you, O Beauty, ever ancient, ever new. Late have I loved you."

In my family, loving classical music was considered to be a sissy thing and an indication of "queerness." I had to become quite literally a closet Beethoven lover, hiding in a closet and listening with earphones on my crystal set to the Sunday broadcasts of the New York Philharmonic. That beauty kept alive in me a hope and trust in the ultimate goodness of life and the existence of a God of beauty and love.

My love for books was another aspect of my childhood that has proved a blessing all my life. Through books I could escape the dreariness, emotional conflicts, and unhappiness of my family into a fantasy world where I could live vicariously the lives of others and thus expand my own horizons a thousandfold. During the summer months, I went with my sister, Marion, to the public library on Utica Street near Jefferson Avenue. Every trip I took out three or four books, which I read voraciously within two or three days.

My stepmother, Katie, who brought a peasant outlook on life with her when she emigrated from the west of Ireland, thought that my reading was a waste of time that would ruin my eyesight and ill prepare me for the job market in that time of Depression. She said to me many times a day, "Wurra, Wurra, when you grow up, who will pay the May rent?" (To this day, every time I pay the May rent, I drink a special toast to the memory of Katie.) I found out later that in the west of Ireland the absentee landlords demanded that the cottagers pay the annual rent in May in the hope the tenants would not have the money after a harsh winter. Consequently, the tenants could be thrown out of their cottages to be homeless on the roads or go to the state-operated poorhouse, where no priest would be allowed to enter to distribute communion or give the last rites.

My stepmother all her life was in terror of ending up in a poorhouse, which she equated with hell. Her fear made it extremely difficult and painful for the family, when her health failed, to place Katie in a nursing home. In fact, she demanded that it was my sister's duty to leave the convent, come home, and take care of her. Already too crippled with arthritis to be able to take care of Katie, Sis refused to go home, but Katie made her go through hell, accusing her of not loving her and of being an ingrate.

My stepmother always urged me to go out in the backyard and help my older brothers, Tom and Charles, fix the motors of the used cars they collected and attempted to restore. But I was always a klutz when it came to working with my hands and felt no interest whatsoever in the workings of the internal combustion engine. Like many gay men, I also felt an absolute horror of getting my hands dirty with grease. My brother Tom, in contrast, took great delight in getting a car running again. On one occasion he invited Katie and me to go for ice cream in a car he just got running. I was riding in the rumble seat. Halfway to the ice cream shop, the engine fell out on the street, to Tom's acute embarrassment.

Each night at my bedtime when I said good night to Katie and my father, she would search me for books and order me to turn off the light and go directly to sleep. I concealed my books on a dumbwaiter and, when I got upstairs, pulled them up, made a tent of the bedclothes, and read my beloved books with a flashlight. Frequently, I read until the light of dawn appeared in my bedroom window. I guess this method of dealing with what I judged was unreasonable authority served me in good stead in future years for my dealings with authorities in the church and the Jesuit order.

My stepmother felt that reading would never equip me for making a living, but there would always be employment for a competent mechanic. When it came time for me to go to high school, I, of course, wanted to go to a liberal arts high school and then go on to college. Neither of my parents had any education beyond learning to read and write in grammar school. My father had to leave school and go to work full-time on the farm when he was twelve years old. My parents insisted that I apply for entrance to Burgardt High School, a school that specialized in preparing young men to be airplane mechanics. One of the items on the entrance application form was: List the titles of any books you read this summer. I remember listing about twenty books. When the admissions official came by my desk and saw my book list, he asked me, "Did you read all these books?"

"Yes," I said, "and many others whose titles I can't remember." I realized later that many of the books I listed were books ordinarily assigned for reading in the junior or senior year of high school. The admissions officer took my application and tore it up.

"This school is meant for those who don't read," he declared. "You belong in a liberal arts high school." My parents were disappointed but agreed to let me apply for entrance to St. Joseph's Collegiate Institute, a liberal arts high school run by the Christian Brothers.

The young men who went to St. Joseph's in 1938 were, for the most part, from Irish, Italian, and Polish blue-collar families. Their parents expected the school to emphasize discipline, with education as a secondary objective. Apart from a few friendly and supportive brothers, I found the atmosphere in the school oppressive and, once again, fear-based. My first year in high school, I was still dressed in knickers and long stockings. All the other boys already wore long pants, the sign of adulthood.

An event that took place more than fifty-five years ago on one of my first days in high school still haunts my memory. I was a scared, lonely thirteen-year-old, starved for affection. One day I was putting my books in a locker in the basement when, suddenly, someone—I never knew who—came around the corner and caught me from behind in a bear hug for a fleeting moment and then disappeared. I shall never forget the profound pleasure I felt in that affectionate and erotic hug. I spent the rest of that year putting books in my locker and taking them out again in hopes of the return of the mysterious hugger, but to no avail.

While I was in high school, my sexuality became a conscious and all-consuming reality in my life. I believe I reached puberty and masturbated for the first time in my junior year, when I was sixteen years old. Of course, there was no such thing as sex education those days at home or at school. All I knew about sex, I learned from my peers. The first time I heard how babies were conceived, it all sounded so dirty and dehumanized that I was sure my schoolmates were lying. The only other source of information I had was the occasional piece of pornography that was passed around the classroom. The result of that introduction to sex was total alienation from my body and its sexual dimension as radically evil and disgusting.

In the religion class, we were taught that all sexual pleasure as such apart from marriage was serious sin. In fact, I remember reading a pamphlet by a Father Kelly, S.J., who claimed that to take the slightest pleasure in any sexual thought or fantasy would be mortal sin. It amazes me today how much psychic damage was done to us in the name of religion and the church. I was delighted many years later with the message I heard when I was in clinical training to become a psychotherapist. The psychiatrist told us that when we interview a new client we should always take a sexual history. He remarked that if the client was capable of guilt-free masturbation, we could be sure we were dealing with a fairly healthy person who was at home with his or her body and its sexuality. If the client told us that he or she never masturbated, then we could be sure we were dealing with someone who was seriously ill.

Once I experienced the sexual pleasure of masturbation, I became compulsively involved with it. For the next twenty years, I was in a constant struggle to try to suppress my sexual desires. The more I prayed to get control of my sex drive, the more compulsive it became. My fear of God and of Jesus was based in part on the distorted image I grew up with concerning Jesus' role as judge. During high school, I was exposed to many a retreat master's traditional talk on sin, death, judgment, and eternal hellfire, often all too similar to the sermon on hell that James Joyce recalls in *Portrait of the Artist as a Young Man*. Basically that talk, designed to scare us into being good ("good" being equated with avoiding sexual pleasure) went like this: John and Mary, two good, sinless, Catholic teenagers, daily communicants, went to the high school prom together. Following the dance, they parked in lovers' lane and made out in the back seat of John's father's car. When they pulled out onto the highway on the way home—crash! They had a fatal highway accident and, because they died unrepentant in mortal sin, they went straight to hell for all eternity. There followed a half-hour of gruesome, detailed descriptions of what it meant to spend eternity being burned in hellfire. There are so many distortions and misconceptions about the nature of God, sin, and judgment in this scenario that it is difficult to know where to begin to straighten things out.

Needless to say, this kind of preaching confirmed the hold on me that the image of God as a god of fear had. Every time I had a sexual fantasy or compulsively masturbated (and at times in my adolescent years that could be several times a day), I could not be at peace until I got to confession and begged God's forgiveness. At one point, I started to go to confession daily, reciting the words of the Act of Contrition: "O my God, I am heartily sorry for having offended thee, because I dread the loss of heaven and the pains of hell." The words went on "but most of all because I love you, my God, who art all good and deserving of all my love!" but I did not. My primary motive for going to confession was fear. The concept of loving a god of whom I stood in terror was incomprehensible. Again, perfect fear casts out all love. After a while,

I began to doubt my own sincerity; how could I be truly repentant if I could predict that I would sin again tomorrow? This led to a state close to despair. But my devotion to Mary, my mother and Jesus' mother, saved me from despair and the loss of faith.

Add to the antisexual attitude of my family and church my own awareness that my sexual attraction, even in early childhood, was always to the male, which made sex doubly evil and doubly hopeless because I could never know the relief of being able to legitimately express my sexuality in the context of marriage.

In those times of economic Depression, every member of the family was expected to bring in some money to keep food on the table and pay the rent. My first job, when I was ten, was delivering newspapers on the east side of Buffalo. I still remember vividly delivering the *Buffalo Evening News* with the headlines announcing the German invasion of Poland and the outbreak of war between Germany and England. During the long Buffalo winters, I pulled my sled piled high with newspapers through the snowstorms and cold. My second job was as a butcher's assistant in a meat market. My job was to clean and degut the freshly killed chickens. The hours were long. On Saturdays, I worked from six in the morning until ten at night. I hated every minute of it. This was the only job I had from which I was fired. The butcher told me it was obvious that I was never meant to be a meat cutter, and truer words were never spoken. But that firing confirmed Katie's fear of my inability "to pay the May rent."

I held several other jobs in high school. I worked at a jewelry store on Jefferson Avenue, where I washed the windows and the owner's car and delivered jewelry and watches downtown to be remounted or repaired. My best job was at Scott's roller skating rink on Main Street. I reported to work at six in the evening, checked in coats until the skating began, served at the food and soda counter until closing around eleven, checked out the coats, cleaned up the food and soda counter, and then walked the two miles home about one o'clock in the morning. I had to be up at six to go to mass and be at school by eight. I also worked at the rink all day Saturday and Sunday for a magnificent salary of fifteen dollars a week. After I turned my paycheck over to Katie, I got my weekly allowance of two dollars.

My final job before entering the army was at Sears Roebuck. I worked first in the menswear section in work clothes. Many of my customers were Rosie the Riveter types buying work clothes for their jobs in the defense industries. Frequently, when I asked them what inseam length they needed, to my acute embarrassment they would spread their legs and say, "Measure me!" In the spring, to my great relief, I was transferred to the garden department and became an instant expert on grass seed and flowers. From early childhood, I always loved gardening and gathered all the information I could about plants and flowers. This knowledge would serve me well in novitiate and in later life. To this day, my favorite way to relax is working in my flower garden.

4

Prisoner of War

In 1942, while I was a senior in high school, World War II was in full swing, and, one by one, my brothers were drafted. Chuck was assigned to the army post office in Birmingham, England, Tom ended up with the air force in New Guinea, and Francis worked as a military policeman in Italy.

The brothers at St. Joseph's Collegiate Institute allowed the senior class to take the final high school state regents exams in December instead of waiting until June. I managed to pass and enrolled at Canisius College in January of 1942. It was my first experience with the intelligence and spirituality of the Jesuit teachers, and in those few months at Canisius I was deeply impressed.

That year, the D-day invasion of Normandy was being planned, but the army brass were distressed by their shortage of young manpower. Because they knew that the voters, especially the women, would not tolerate the draft age being lowered to seventeen, Congress set up a program called ASTP (army specialized training program). To this day, I am convinced that it was nothing more than a hoax to bring seventeen-year-old boys into the army. The word spread in the colleges that the army was setting up an officer training program for engineers. Seventeen-year-old college students were invited to take a competitive exam to qualify for the program. My Jesuit teachers urged us to take part. We should have become suspicious when everybody passed. I was ordered to enlist in the army and, in September, was sent to Cornell University to begin taking the fundamental classes in math and science. As I left Buffalo's train station, I plucked a hair from the stuffed buffalo in the lobby and put it in my wallet for good luck, according to local custom. By the end of the war, the buffalo was hairless and replaced by a bronze statue.

The exquisite beauty of the autumn foliage is one of my most vivid mem-

ories of that fall on the Cornell campus. Another was hearing the campus car-
illon playing "Oh My Darling Clementine" at noon, instead of the Angelus.
It seemed so pagan to me. One day while we were waiting in a chow line, I
was explaining some theological concept to a fellow student next to me, when
someone spun me around and shouted at me, "If there is a God, let him strike
me dead!" It was the first time I met John Thornton, who has remained a good
friend for the past fifty-five years. John had just graduated from Regis High
School in Manhattan (a scholarship school run by the Jesuits for the best and
the brightest from the parochial system) and was an aggressive atheist. I tried
to explain to him that, if God did exist and was a God of love, he could not
fulfill John's request without acting contrary to God's own nature.

In December, we were told by the program administrators that ASTP had
been poorly and hastily organized, so they had to make a change in plans. We
would be first sent for basic training as infantry soldiers at Fort Benning, Geor-
gia. Then, once we completed that, we were told, we would return to classes.
The very day our basic training ended, however, Congress announced that
they had discontinued the ASTP, which they had probably intended to do all
along. There we were, thousands of bright seventeen-year-olds, ready to be
cannon fodder. I was assigned to the 347th Regiment of the 87th Infantry Division in Fort Jackson, South Carolina, which was preparing to ship out to Europe.

I was a terrible misfit in the infantry. I was terrified of guns. The first time
I fired a rifle, I wet my pants in fear. I felt totally inadequate to the physical
demands made on me. The captain in charge of our platoon in basic training
asked me, "Does your mother know you're away from home yet?"

I have some pleasant memories of that period, especially the times I spent
with my best friends in service, John Thornton and Samuel Weisberg, who
were my frequent companions. Many times I sat composing poetry with Sam
at the rifle range. Once we celebrated the feast of Purim, which honors the
deliverance of the Jews from potential extermination in Persia, by reading the
book of Esther in the Old Testament, hissing the name of the villain, Haman.
We ate special pastries Sam's mother sent to us.

One time when Sam's mother came to visit us at Fort Jackson, she learned
that I was on KP (kitchen patrol) duty. She went to my company sergeant and
told him that she was my mother and had come all the way from New York

City. She convinced him to issue me a pass for the weekend. The three of us—Sam, his mother, and I—spent the weekend together in the city of Columbia, South Carolina. After the war, I brought her to see the "miraculously preserved" body of Mother Cabrini in a church in the Bronx. She was deeply impressed and expressed the hope someday to take me to see the miraculously preserved body of Stalin in the Kremlin.

I managed to get myself into serious conflict during training. We were shown indoctrination films designed to make us "hate the enemy." An officer gave a talk in which he stated, "Unless you learn to hate the enemy, you cannot make a good soldier!" When he asked if there were any questions, I raised my hand. I told him that I was a Catholic and a Christian and I could not in conscience hate the enemy. I quoted scripture: "Love your enemies and pray for those who persecute you" (Matthew 5:44). I held up as a model the Jesuit students in Spain who fought in their civil war. Every morning before going into combat, they received communion and prayed for the souls of all their enemies whom they would kill that day. The next day I was called in for interrogation by "army intelligence." I received a red mark on my record as a troublemaker and was refused the standard raise in rank to private first class given to all privates who completed basic training. It is interesting to note that at the end of the war, Congress passed a law raising all former POWs one grade in rank: captains became majors, majors became colonels. So it was only by an act of Congress that I went from private to private first class, with a five-dollar-a-month increase in my paycheck. The officer who informed me of this assured me that he didn't think I deserved this raise.

Finally, in September 1944, we boarded the *Queen Elizabeth* to set out for Europe. More than fifteen thousand men were stuffed into every nook and cranny of that luxury liner. Tiers of sleeping bunks were built into the first-class swimming pool, and mine was tenth up.

Sam, John, and I decided to entertain the troops while we were still in the harbor in New York. We sang the music from the opera *Carmen*, and I sang the title role. In my youthful tenor voice, which was trained by singing in the choir of Our Lady of Loreto Church in Buffalo, my rendition of "L'Amour" was, I believe, the best I ever did and well received by the assembled troops.

While still in sight of the Statue of Liberty, I began feeling seasick. I had been put on guard duty near a kitchen. The greasy smells from the kitchen, together with the evasive actions of the huge liner after it left the harbor (it continually zigzagged as it crossed the ocean to avoid any submarine lying in ambush), were too much for me. I was desperately ill for the next seven days and wanted to die.

After what seemed like an eternity, we finally arrived in the Firth of Forth near Glasgow, and I was intensely aware of the beautiful park lands surrounding the firth. We were taken ashore and packed into trains, which took us to our training base at Congleton in Cheshire. I was fascinated by the beauty of the countryside. In Congleton, we lived in what was once the Marsuma cigar mill. All of us became infested with lice and had to be deloused.

My friend Sam and I befriended a local family and on occasion went to their house for tea. They had one daughter, then about ten, with whom Sam has remained friends to this day and visits on his frequent trips to England. I bought a bicycle to perform my duties as a messenger, but within the week we were ordered to France. I gave the bicycle as a gift to the family who befriended us. When I returned home after the war, I discovered that my English friends had sold the bicycle and sent the money to my parents in Buffalo.

In England, my big adventure was visiting my brother Charles at the army post office in Birmingham. I hitchhiked my way there on a three-day pass. I was amused at my drivers' attempts to save gas by driving up hills and then letting their cars coast down the other side. Charles was billeted with a middle-class family in a suburb of Birmingham. Talking with the woman of that house was my first real encounter with class prejudice. She greeted me warmly and told me it was a privilege to have such a gentleman as my brother in her house. "After all," she said, "this war is such a terrible thing. My son is in the army and has to hobnob with truck drivers and that ilk." Afterward, Chuck explained that he'd shown her a picture of his house and car and she assumed his family was upper middle class like hers. Ironically, Chuck was a truck driver for the post office in Buffalo for a time.

That night, we went to the Horse and Whistle Pub, where we were made welcome by the locals. I don't remember very much of what happened. English ale was too strong for me. Chuck tells me that at one point I got up on a table and regaled the whole pub with my rendition of an Irish ballad, "The Rose of Tralee." When Chuck took me home, I remember the room was spinning around before I dropped off to sleep.

A few days after I returned to my army post, my regiment boarded a train to the coast and then boarded ships to cross to France. On the ship, I spoke to a soldier who had been in combat, was wounded twice, and was now returning to combat for the third time. The depth of his depression and despair was extraordinary. We landed at Calais, on the coast of France directly across the English Channel, and the ruins of that port city were my first sight of the destructiveness of the war.

Once in France, we set up our encampment in some farm fields in Normandy. Sam and I disobeyed orders and sneaked out to visit the nearby town. Sam knew some French, so we were able to converse. As we came to the village, we heard a female voice singing exquisitely. Following the sound, we found a young girl singing as she washed laundry at a fountain. We visited the local church, and I was profoundly moved by Christ's presence in the sacrament. Afterward, Sam remarked that I made him feel that a third party was in the sanctuary with us. The pastor invited us in for a glass of wine. We noticed that he had portraits of three war leaders on his wall—Churchill, Roosevelt, and Stalin. We asked why Stalin, and he responded that he was covering all his bases because he was not yet sure who would win. He mentioned that our regimental commander was billeted in the priest house and should be back any minute, so we quickly took our leave.

Our final stop was at a farmhouse. The farmer also invited us in for a glass of wine. He told us stories of living under German occupation. By that time, it was becoming dark, so we started walking back to our encampment. We had gone only a short distance when the farmer came running frantically to catch us, carrying my M1 rifle in his hands. I had left it leaning against his kitchen wall. The farmer was frightened that he would be accused of stealing it. That cardinal sin of leaving my rifle behind, a crime punishable by court-martial, is a clear indication of my total failure to be able to identify myself as a soldier.

Again by train, we moved up to the Saar basin at Metz and were told that we of the 87th Division would join the Third Army under the command of General George Patton.

My infantry outfit went into combat on a dark night in mid-December of 1944. We marched up to the front line in total darkness in a straight line, each of us with the right hand on the shoulder of the man in front. There we replaced, man for man, the members of the Yankee Division, which had been in combat continuously since D-day. There was another line of soldiers passing us. Suddenly, I heard the voice of my poet friend, Samuel Weisberg. I called out to him, and he responded. We wished each other well, our voices growing fainter as our columns moved farther apart in the dark.

I found out after the war that our line was only a short distance away from the border of Germany at the Saar basin. We were one of the first infantry divisions to try to penetrate into Germany. We slept that night in the foxholes dug by the men we replaced. Artillery shells shrieked through the night sky, their explosions lighting the skyline ahead of and behind us. I slept fitfully, feeling cold, lonely, and scared out of my wits.

At dawn, our officers lined us up in combat formation and told us that at their signal we were to advance across a valley toward the German lines. Just before moving up to the front lines, our supply officers realized that we would need galoshes to wear over our shoes, which were not waterproof. A truck filled with galoshes came to the camp and dumped them out. We were told to pick out a pair that fit. Rather than take part in the melee of soldiers searching for their size, I sat back, deciding to take whatever was left. To my surprise, all that remained were two left boots. I went into combat with a constant tendency to swerve to the left.

I was second ammunition bearer in a mortar squad. I went into combat with my own carbine and backpack and more than a hundred pounds of mortar ammunition in a bandolier draped over my shoulders. I still remember the beauty of that late fall morning, the blueness of the sky, the rolling green fields, and songbirds flying overhead. I was a young man just turned eighteen years of age and passionately in love with life as we set out to kill or be killed. We had proceeded only a few hundred yards down the hillside when German artillery shells began landing in our midst.

What happened that day more than fifty years ago is now very confused in my memory. Every time I heard the shriek of an incoming artillery shell, I had to dive for cover face down in the mud. Each time, the bandolier of mortar shells flipped up and struck me on the back of the head, driving my face deeper into the mud, and each time my helmet rolled off into the field. By the time I struggled to my feet, retrieved my helmet, and started off again, walking clumsily in my two left boots, another shell came screaming in. After what seemed like hours of walking and falling, my mortar squad finally located a

German machine-gun nest on the hillside ahead of us and fired on it. As we were firing, several Tiger tanks came around the hill and veered directly toward us at full speed with their cannon barrels swinging in our direction. Four or five of us in the mortar squad raced up the side of the hill and took refuge in the machine-gun nest we had just fired on. On the way, a young soldier I had met at Cornell came running past me toward the rear lines, terror and agony in his face. I saw that shrapnel had almost torn off his left leg. He was leaving a trail of blood as he ran.

The German Tiger tank stopped at the foot of the hill and began raking the hillside with machine-gun fire. Every time we tried to stand up, there was a burst of machine-gun fire just over our heads. As trained infantrymen, we knew well what would follow. While keeping us pinned down so that we could not return fire, a German soldier would crawl up to within throwing distance and toss a grenade into our midst. We conferred and decided that the only choice open to us other than death was to surrender. After a quick prayer to God to protect me, I took off my T-shirt and stood up waving it in the air. Sure enough, I saw the German soldier, potato-masher grenade in hand only about twenty feet away. He stood up and waved us down the hill, keeping his machine pistol trained on us. A group of German soldiers surrounded us when we reached the bottom of the hill. They disarmed us and helped themselves to our gloves and American cigarettes. In broken English, they told us they had just been transferred from the Russian front and we were their first American prisoners. They spoke about how happy they were to be dealing with Americans instead of Russians and how they expected that, as soon as we encountered the Russian army, they would be our allies in the ensuing war with Russia. Over the next several months as a prisoner, this was the friendliest encounter I had with German soldiers.

Little did I know then the role Sam played shortly after my capture. He risked his life to go out into no-man's-land and search through the dead to ascertain that I was not among them. He sent a letter to my parents that kept their hopes up that I was still alive during the next six months while I was officially reported "missing in action."

After a brief conversation, our captors began to send us back to a prisoner collection center behind the lines. I was aware that, to take us back and return, they would have to pass through the American artillery barrage twice.

To my surprise and dismay, instead of sending us all back under one guard, they began to assign each of us prisoners a guard and send us off at intervals, one by one. I had heard rumors that on occasion, rather than expose themselves to the danger of passing through the artillery barrage, the Germans would shoot the prisoner and claim he tried to escape. Walking down the road with the certainty that I was about to be shot, we came upon a roadside shrine, very common in the Saar, of the crucified Christ. I asked my guard for permission to say a prayer. As he leaned on his rifle and smoked one of my cigarettes, I fell to my knees, made an act of contrition, and asked God to protect me and save me from death. I think that that was one of the most earnest prayers of my whole life. I surrendered myself totally to God's mercy, and obviously God had other plans for me.

When I rose to my feet, I fully expected a bullet in the back of my head. Instead, my guard marched me through the artillery barrage and turned me over to an officer in charge of the prisoner collection center. Under interrogation, I gave that officer my name, rank, and serial number: John McNeill, Private, 12238624. He was quite surprised to learn that I was only a private, saying I was the only private he had ever met among the prisoners. I had two books in my backpack. One was my Roman Missal with prayers and scripture readings for each day of the year, the other was Thomas Mann's novella *Tonio Kröger,* in the original German, a book assigned by my German teacher, Father Tom Brady, at Canisius College. (Canisius was founded by German Jesuits from Berlin who had been ousted from Germany during Bismarck's Kulturkampf.) The officer kept my copy of *Tonio Kröger* but returned my missal to me. That missal served a variety of purposes during the next few months. Each morning, I fervently read the prayers and scripture passages for that day and then, because the latrines in prison camp had no toilet paper, tore the page out and made pragmatic use of it.

The next day, we were marched farther into Germany to another interrogation point. As we passed through the streets of Saarbrücken, I saw nuns, wearing habits similar to the one my sister wore back in Buffalo, peering at us with curiosity out the windows of a Catholic school. When we reached our destination, about twenty of us were sealed into a dark room with no food and water. Over a loudspeaker for the next twenty-four hours they played continuously, "I'm Dreaming of a White Christmas" sung by Bing Crosby. To this day

I can't tolerate hearing that song without feeling depressed. The double memory of my mother's funeral wreath replacing the Christmas wreath when I was four and that night of "White Christmas" torture in 1944 has always given Christmas, despite its joyous message, an overcast of tragedy and sadness throughout my life.

Eventually, we were called one by one to a warm, well-lighted room with a cheerful blaze in the fireplace. I was offered a hot chocolate to drink by a kindly looking white-haired officer, who asked questions about when I left the United States, on what boat, when did we land in Normandy, what was my commanding officer's name, and so on. Once again, I dutifully responded with name, rank, and serial number. I began to worry that, even if they tortured me for the answers, I really did not know my commanding officer's name or the date we left New York. Fortunately, being only a private, I was small fry, so the officer tossed me back.

Later that day, we were loaded into a railroad boxcar and taken to the freight yard in the city of Kaiserslautern. An air raid broke out, and we were taken from the boxcar and herded into a storage shed at the side of the tracks. Sitting with my back to a partition in the shed, I noticed prisoners on the other side of the partition. Looking through a crack, I saw a group of Russian soldiers. One was looking back at me. He smiled and asked if I was American. When I responded yes, he passed me a Russian cigarette, probably one of his last, as a gift. I often thought of that encounter after the war, amid all the paranoid anti-Russian feeling of the Cold War. My first face-to-face meeting with the dreaded Russians was one of smiles, mutual respect, and a generous and unselfish gift.

That night there was another air raid. I was lying on the ground and trying to sleep while listening to the air raid sirens and the German antiaircraft guns that surrounded the railroad yard. Suddenly, there was a loud bang and a sound of something ricocheting among the rafters. Then I was struck in the side; it felt like someone hit me with a two-by-four. I jumped up and asked who hit me, but the rest of the prisoners told me to go back to sleep. Nothing further happened until dawn, when I woke up to find myself cuddled around a live antiaircraft shell that had failed to explode. I backed away in terror, and the guards ordered us out of the storage shack. Once again I had come close to death, but God had other plans.

We were taken by truck to a major prison camp outside the city of Limburg. The camp was full of American soldiers, mostly eighteen- and nineteen-year-olds who were captured in the Battle of the Bulge. We realized immediately that this POW camp, with large red crosses painted on the roofs of the barracks, was built around V2 rocket-launching platforms. Each evening at sundown, we watched armed rockets climb into the twilight sky on their way to England or the coastal cities under Allied control.

On Christmas Eve, the Germans served us prisoners a special meal that included a piece of Spam, the only time we were served meat in the several months that I was a prisoner. As I was eating, I noticed a red glow coming in through the shuttered windows. I realized, when the bombs started falling, that the glow was the marker flares dropped by a wave of Allied bombers and that the V2 launching platforms were their target. Our guards ran to previously prepared air-raid ditches outside the camp, where they could be relatively safe from the bombs and shoot down any prisoners attempting to escape.

A few minutes later, bombs began to rain down on the camp. Some of the barracks sustained direct hits, and all the prisoners inside were killed. I was lucky to escape without injury. I have no idea how many young American soldiers died that night. The next day those of us who were still alive and capable of walking were loaded into boxcars without food or water. We were so packed in that we had to take turns sitting or standing. There was no toilet; we had to defecate or urinate where we sat or stood. That boxcar was to be our home for the next ten days as we made our way across Germany to Leukenwalde, south of Berlin. That ten-day trip was one of the most painful times of my life. The temperature was below freezing. After a few days without water, our thirst was excruciating. I survived by licking the frozen condensation off the nailheads on the wall until my tongue bled. The inability to stretch out and rest was torture.

During a stop in a freight yard, we caught the attention of a slave laborer and asked him to fill, at a nearby water pump, a helmet liner that we passed out to him. As he lifted the helmet liner full of water to the window, a guard came around the boxcar and struck the liner to the ground and threatened to shoot the laborer. In anguish, we watched the precious water soak into the ground. Several prisoners who had been badly wounded in the bombing died en route shortly after.

Eventually, we arrived at the prison camp in Leukenwalde, Stammlager 12A. The guards lined us up and marched us into the camp, but I was too weak to keep up. A guard beat me with a belt to make me stay in line. They processed us, took our pictures, and assigned us each a prison number; mine was 097593. But once we arrived in camp, a great surprise awaited us, a surprise I feel confident saved my life. There was a group of British prisoners in the camp. Captured at Dunkirk, they had been prisoners for more than five years but had an amazing esprit de corps, much in the same manner as Kurt Vonnegut described in his account of his prisoner-of-war experience in *Slaughterhouse-Five*. They were receiving care packages from the Red Cross. They brewed a big kettle of hot tea made with their precious tea rations and had it ready for us as we arrived. That beautiful tea, the first drink I had had in ten days, helped open my stomach, which had closed, and allowed me to swallow some solid food. To this day I feel enormous gratitude to those British soldiers and admiration for their spirit after their long years of imprisonment.

The British were hopeful that the war would end soon and they could return to family and friends in England. One soldier kept talking about going to Buckingham Palace to see the queen. An insensitive American from Tennessee, getting tired of all the talk about the queen, responded, "Oh, fuck the Queen!" I expected a new outbreak of the American Revolution. But the British soldier looked at the American with amazement and with beautiful understatement replied: "I say, Mac, 'Fuck the Queen?!' You *cahn't* even get *neah* her!"

After our rescue from starvation by the British, we were moved to our own section of the camp. The camp was home also to several thousand Russian prisoners. Typhoid was rampant. When the news of the Battle of the Bulge reached the camp, the German guards boasted that they were winning the war. As long as the prisoners had had some hope that the war would end soon, there were only one or two deaths each day. In the weeks following that news, deaths increased to between ten and twenty a day. We Americans had been inoculated stateside against typhoid so we were sent into the Russian side of the camp to collect the bodies and take them for burial outside the camp.

Our food ration was drastically reduced to a small potato and some turnip soup once a day. I was starving. My weight fell from one hundred and forty pounds to less than eighty pounds. As soon as I began to starve, all I and the other prisoners could think about was food. We spent hours torturing ourselves and each other with descriptions of Thanksgiving Day feasts. One soldier from West Virginia described in great detail hunting down and capturing possum, which he would then fatten up and his mother would bake and serve slabs of possum fat to the children. My daily dream consisted of walking down Main Street in Buffalo and going into Freddie's Donut Shop. (His store had the first automatic door I ever went through. When I reached out to push it open, I fell flat on my face.) Once inside, in my dream, I bought two dozen donuts—jelly, cream, honey-glazed, crullers, chocolate. Outside, I sat on the curb and ate and ate and ate. I always woke up from that dream hungrier than ever.

Prior to being in prison camp, I was always preoccupied with sexual thoughts and desires. I seemed to have a very high sexual drive. But after being a prisoner for a few weeks, all sexual thoughts and desires disappeared, not to appear again until I began to eat regularly once more.

One day as I was kneeling and washing out bedpans in the Russian section of the camp, I prayed, "Lord! I don't want to die so young. Please give me some food!" Just as I was saying that prayer, an elderly guard came up to me, poked me with his elbow, and gave me some crusts of bread. I was astonished at the quick response God gave my prayer. It made another crack in my understanding of God as a god of fear. I felt that God was close to me and that my prayers were being heard.

Years after the war, I read Viktor Frankl's *Man's Search for Meaning* (New York: Washington Square Press, 1985) and found that book the most profound and enlightening reflection on my own experience in prison camp. Frankl spent several years in a concentration camp. His experiences of savagery and torture as a Jew in a concentration camp went way beyond my own experience as a prisoner of war, so I do not want even to hint at a comparison. The lesson Frankl drew from his experience became the basis for his new theory of psychotherapeutic healing, which he called *logotherapy*, or therapy through meaning.

Frankl writes, "Those who know how close the connection is between the state of mind of a man—his courage and hope, or lack of them—and the state of immunity of his body, will understand that the sudden loss of hope and courage can have a deadly effect." Frankl reports that in the week between Christmas 1944 and New Year's Day 1945, the same week I was crossing Germany in a boxcar on my way to Leukenwalde, the death rate increased beyond all previous experience in his camp. The majority of the prisoners had lived in the naive hope that they would be home again at Christmas. When news of the Allies' defeat at the Battle of the Bulge arrived, the prisoners lost courage and hope, and disappointment overcame them. Their powers of resistance weakened, and a great number of them losing the will to live, died.

"Hunger, humiliation, fear, and deep anger at injustice are rendered tolerable by closely guarded images of beloved persons, by religion, by a grim sense of humor and even by glimpses of the healing beauties of nature—a tree or a sunset." Frankl's experience in concentration camp led him to the conclusion: "Any attempt to restore a prisoner's inner strength had first to succeed in showing him the meaning of his suffering and some future goal (some transcending reason to live). As Nietzsche said, 'He who has a *why* to live for, can bear almost any *how*.'"

Although the prisoners had almost no control over the circumstances in their lives, they never lost that inner freedom—the freedom to choose how they would react to their circumstances and to take responsibility for that reaction. "When a man finds that it is his destiny to suffer, he will have to accept his suffering as his task, his single and unique task. He will have to acknowledge the fact that even in suffering he is unique and alone in the universe. No one can relieve him of his suffering or suffer in his place. His unique opportunity lies in the way he bears his burden. Human life," Frankl wrote, "under any circumstances, never ceases to have a meaning, and this infinite meaning of life is not negated by suffering and dying."

I know that the strong religious faith that I brought into prison camp with me was a source of inner strength and courage for me. Frequently, however, I did not live up to the values that faith taught me. Most of the time, I was reduced to being selfishly centered in my own survival and ready to steal or do whatever I had to in order to survive.

The German guards tried to organize food distribution in the American camp, but the prisoners did not trust each other. There were continual disputes and fighting. In exasperation, the guards decided to place the day's ration of bread or potatoes in the middle of the camp and allow us to fight for our share. I remember grabbing a piece of bread and running with it until I had consumed it.

In the middle of this chaos, one example of courage based in faith impressed me so deeply that it influenced the rest of my life. A group of us American prisoners were sent out on a work detail to a farm where SS officers were raising mink. Our job was to chop firewood. An Eastern European slave laborer was working close to me, mixing a mash for the animals. The mash included real potatoes and carrots. I could not take my eyes off the food. He must have detected my starving condition, for, when the guard's back was turned, he reached into the mash and threw me a potato. If the guard had caught him the laborer would almost certainly have been killed. I quickly hid the potato in my jacket and tried to signal a thanks to him. His only response was to make the sign of the cross. That sign of the cross was like a flash of lightning on a dark night. Here was a man who was willing to risk his life to feed me, a stranger, and he found that courage and his freedom from fear in his religious faith. I date my vocation to the priesthood from that moment. My constant prayer from then on was that God would grant me the courage to never be ruled by fear: "Grant me the wisdom, Lord, to know your will and the courage to be able to do it!"

I became intensely aware that evil's primary instrument in this world is fear. If I could attain with God's grace a profound awareness of God's personal love for me, I could be freed from the personal grip that fear had on my life. I always loved the Advent collect that read: "Lord! Remove the blindness that cannot know you; relieve the fear that hides me from your face!" On nearly every other page of the New Testament, we find the words "Do not be afraid!" I wanted to be free enough to reach out, no matter what the cost, to help someone who needed me. I knew that my vocation and ministry would demand of me the fearlessness and courage to reach out and share the suffering of others. I envisioned my future ministry as holding a dying soldier in my arms and absorbing his pain and fear so that he could die in peace.

Kurt Vonnegut, in *Slaughterhouse-Five* (New York: Delacorte Press/Seymour Lawrence, 1968), quotes a manuscript written by an American, Howard Campbell, who was a member of the German Ministry of Propaganda, a report on the behavior in Germany of American enlisted men as prisoners of war. I do not know if this manuscript is fact or fiction. In either case, it contains an interesting insight into American psychology, which, although exaggerated, has a grain of truth:

America is the wealthiest nation on Earth, but its people are mainly poor, and poor Americans are urged to hate themselves. . . . It is in fact a crime for an American to be poor, even though America is a nation of poor. Every other nation has folk traditions of men who were poor but extremely wise and virtuous, and therefore more estimable than anyone with power and gold. No such tales are told by the American poor. They mock themselves and glorify their betters. . . . Americans, like human beings everywhere, believe many things that are obviously untrue. Their most destructive untruth is that it is very easy for any American to make money. They will not acknowledge how, in fact, hard money is to come by, and therefore, those who have no money blame and blame and blame themselves. This inward blame has been a treasure for the rich and powerful, who have had to do less for their poor, publicly and privately, than any other ruling class. . . . Many novelties have come from America. The most startling of these, a thing without precedent, is a mass of undignified poor. They do not love one another because they do not love themselves. Once this is understood, the disagreeable behavior of American enlisted men in German prisons ceases to be a mystery. A prison administrator dealing with captured American enlisted men for the first time should be warned: Expect no brotherly love, even between brothers. There will be no cohesion between the individuals. Each will be a sulky child who often wishes he were dead.

Campbell told what the German experience with captured American enlisted men had been:

They were known everywhere to be the most self-pitying, least fraternal, and dirtiest of all prisoners of war. They were incapable of concerted action on their own behalf. They despised any leader from among their own number, refused to follow, or even listen to him, on the grounds that he was no better than they were, that he should stop putting on airs.

Politicians of today still take advantage of and nurture this self-rejection of the American poor in the name of welfare reform.

Because I was the only American in our camp to have some knowledge of German, I was frequently called on to translate for the guards. Once, some sympathetic civilians threw loaves of bread over the fence to us starving prisoners. The guards saw them. The officer in charge called us all out, placed a pistol at my head, and demanded that I translate for the other prisoners that they must bring out what had been thrown in to them or he would shoot me. To my great relief, they did show the officer what remained of the bread, and I was let go.

On a few occasions, some acts of humaneness from some guards did occur. Once, for example, a compassionate elderly guard brought us some pea soup, my favorite soup ever since. He told us that he had been a prisoner of war in England in World War I, and he knew what it was like to starve as a prisoner.

Another time our guards, with great self-satisfaction, announced to us prisoners that they would show us a motion picture that evening because they were aware how much Americans loved motion pictures. When we returned from work, they gathered us in an auditorium and treated us to a slapstick comedy film, *Homweg mit Glück*. The film told the story of the unfortunate events surrounding a German peasant's efforts to return home. As the guards laughed heartily at the antics of the hero, we sat there gloomily, unable to understand the German dialogue and listening to the gurgling of our empty stomachs.

We also experienced acts of brutality. We were brought to a freight yard, given pitchforks, and told to shovel coal briquettes out of a boxcar into a wagon. I was too hungry and weak to lift a fork full of coal bricks to throw them over the five-foot-high wall of the boxcar. I sat on the floor and began throwing the coal bricks over the wall one by one. When the guard saw what I was doing he ordered me to stand up and use my pitchfork. In a moment of imprudent courage, I refused to obey, saying, *"Keine essen, keine arbeiten!"* ("No food, no work!") In a rage, the guard attacked me and beat me with the pitchfork.

The commander of our work camp, Leutnant Knopf, was proud of his ability to drive a motorcycle and took great sadistic delight in terrorizing us with it. Several times when we were returning from work detail, he ordered us to line up carefully side by side in a straight line. He positioned a German soldier with a machine gun at one end of the line with strict orders to shoot any of us who fell out of line. Then he began one of his favorite nasty tricks. He circled us in his motorcycle with a side car until he had built up a high speed and then drove directly at us. At the last instant, he tilted his vehicle so that the wheel of the sidecar passed within inches of our faces. He sped right down the line that way threatening us, terrifying us, so that we would react in fear and step back to be shot. Miraculously, though it happened several times, none of us fell victim to his malicious motorcycling.

After we had been on starvation rations for about two weeks, the Germans sent a celebrity to our camp. He was the boxer, Max Schmeling, the man whose boxing career was put to an end by Joe Louis's knockout. In a perfect parallel with Kurt Vonnegut's recounting of Campbell's visit to his camp in Dresden, Max Schmeling came to recruit men for a German military unit, "the American Corps." Schmeling told us that if we resigned our rights as prisoners of war under the Geneva Convention, we could join the German army fighting the Russians, and we would receive the same food rations as the German soldiers. Although the offer was very tempting because we were literally being starved, I realized that to join would be an act of treason and I would rather die of starvation than to go to my death with the sin on my conscience that I had betrayed my country. About half the prisoners signed up. The next day, trucks came and took them away. We never heard of them again.

After two months at Leukenwald, a group of us Americans, who were privates and for the most part privates first class, were rounded up in a work squad and sent into Berlin. The German army, very conscious of rank, had separate camps for commissioned and noncommissioned officers. But according to the Geneva Convention, they could use prisoners with no rank in work squads. In Berlin, we were put to work bringing buckets of water to the roof of tenement buildings to put out fires during the firebombing raids. After the air raids, we were made to dig out bodies from the rubble and take them to the lime pits outside the city. During the night, we were left in barracks on the surface, while the guards slept in bomb shelters. Night after night, we were kept awake by the constant noise of bombs exploding and antiaircraft guns blazing. Fortunately for me, while I was a student at St. Joseph's, the brothers had me memorize a long segment of Coleridge's *Ancient Mariner*, which had these beautiful lines when the mariner was finally granted the gift of sleep:

> Oh sleep! it is a gentle thing,
> Beloved from pole to pole.
> To Mary Queen the praise be given,
> She sent the gentle sleep from heaven
> Which slid into my soul.

After reciting this poem as a prayer two or three times, a great peace settled over me. Despite the explosion of bombs, the shriek of air-raid sirens, and the booming of antiaircraft artillery, I fell sound asleep. Once again Mary heard my prayer and was with me.

Frequently, to calm the people during the raids, the Germans played

Beethoven over public loudspeakers, and I found myself caught up again in the beauty of the music in the midst of terror, destruction, and death.

As the Russian army approached Berlin in April, a group of us prisoners were taken hostage by a German general. We were taken on a march along the Elbe toward Hamburg. I was told by our guards that they were under orders to kill all of us if anything happened to the general.

One day as we marched along a country road, Russian fighter planes began to strafe us. I dived into a culvert to escape the bullets. After the strafing ended, we were ordered to line up on the road, but I found myself stuck in the culvert. I had dived in with my hands at my side and now could not move forward or backward. I panicked and screamed for help while thinking this would be a ridiculous way to perish after all the close brushes with death I had been through. Luckily, a German soldier heard me and pulled me out by my feet, and I rejoined the column of prisoners on the road.

Near the city of Schwerin, in northern Germany east of Hamburg, an SS officer on a motorcycle stopped the column of prisoners and lined us up. He walked down the line, picked out anyone he thought looked Jewish, and ordered them to be executed. It didn't matter if they were Jewish; it was enough for him that they looked Jewish. Many of my friends—Jewish, Italian, and others—were brought to a ditch at the edge of the road and machine-gunned.

As we were marched ahead of the advancing Russian troops, I saw, for the first time, multiple rocket launchers sending salvos of shells into the Russian lines. I also saw for the first time German jet fighters with their incredible speed. I was impressed by the superiority of German weapons.

Our small group of prisoners was liberated on May 2, 1945. We were staying at that time in a farmyard outside the town of Dumhof. The British and American armies had been staying west of the Elbe River and allowing the Russian army to advance against the German army east of the Elbe. The British made the decision to cut off the Russian advance before they arrived at the Atlantic directly across from Britain. So on May 2, an American tank column attached to the British army crossed the Elbe, and about noon they stumbled upon us prisoners. A classmate from Canisius College was riding on the first tank we encountered. They took our guards captive, gave us some food and weapons, told us they had reported our position to headquarters, and then pressed on to cut off the Russian advance.

For the next few days, we were an armed contingent of starving POWs, surrounded on all sides by the German army but officially liberated. We set up perimeter guards and raided local farms to seek food from the terrorized old folks. A group of prisoners came across a freight car filled with Holtz alcohol. Mistaking this wood alcohol for drinking alcohol, several prisoners drank themselves to a horrible death. One striking memory was finding a fourteen-year-old German soldier sitting at the side of the road weeping. When I asked him why he was weeping, he showed me a German newspaper with the headline "*Hitler est Todt!*" "With Hitler dead," he told me, "there is no hope!"

Finally, a convoy of trucks arrived and brought us back to a POW collection point. There we were deloused. As soon as the delousing poison hit me, I felt a shock as a thousand little bugs took a death grip on my body. All the time I had been in prison camp, I had been wearing a Cornell University T-shirt with a red C on it. By this time, what was left of the red C was imprinted on my skin. With great relief, all our prison clothes with the KGF (*Kriegsgefangene*, "prisoner of war") imprinted on the back were tossed into a fire, and we ecstatically enjoyed a shower and shave and the pleasure of fresh clothes. We were flown to Camp Lucky Strike, an American army collection center for liberated prisoners in the west of France. From the window of the airplane, I saw unfolding beneath me the devastation of the towns and countryside, the huge holes left by bombs and artillery, the destroyed buildings. I wondered at the monstrous evil of war with all its death, pain, and destruction, and I prayed to God for peace.

I was to have one more brush with death in Europe. On landing at Camp Lucky Strike, our plane went off the runway and flipped over on its side, and we ex-POWs had to be rescued from the crash, an experience that left me with a profound fear of flying for the rest of my life.

During my brief stay in Camp Lucky Strike, the war in Europe came officially to an end on May 7, 1945, when the Germans agreed to an unconditional surrender. A few days later, I found myself aboard a troop carrier plunging through a rough North Atlantic. I was supremely grateful to God to have come through the war alive. I searched out the most stable spot on the boat and listened to the latest hits being played over the loudspeaker: "Rum and Coca-Cola," "The Chattanooga Choo-Choo," and "A String of Pearls."

When we arrived stateside, after a brief reunion with my parents and a visit with my sister, Sister Sheila, in the convent in Buffalo, I was sent to a rehabilitation hospital at The Dennis, a hotel in Atlantic City, New Jersey. There, I was diagnosed as having beriberi, malnutrition, extensive frostbite on my feet, and yellow jaundice. My greatest problem came from the fact that my stomach had closed. For a long time, I could swallow only liquid foods. When I began to eat solids again, I frequently lost my meal without warning. Once, this happened to me when I went, after dinner, with a Jesuit friend to a Broadway theater to see *Carousel,* much to his and my extreme embarrassment. I overheard nearby members of the audience making nasty comments about "the drunken soldier." For several years after that, I could not dine out. A doctor advised me to smoke after meals to help retention, and smoking became part of my digestive process. After Charlie's first heart attack in 1973, we both had a difficult struggle to free ourselves from addiction to nicotine. Through mutual encouragement, we were able to quit.

Because the war in the Pacific was still going on, there was the threat that if I recovered sufficiently, I could be sent into combat once again. After my discharge from the army hospital in Atlantic City, I was sent to an army camp in Maryland, just outside of Washington, D.C., and assigned to clerical duty. The unconditional surrender of the Japanese on September 2, 1945, brought that threat to an end.

While at army camp in Maryland, I had my first sexual experience. A sergeant invited me out on a double date. The two women worked for the Navy Department in Washington. We stayed overnight, and each of us went to bed with our respective dates. This was my first and only experience of heterosexual sex. I was so nervous, I came immediately. The next day at the barracks, when I went to the latrine to urinate, I felt the most excruciating pain in my penis. I was sure I had caught the venereal disease the army training films had depicted. I reported to the infirmary and told the doctor I had contracted a venereal disease. He examined me and asked me when I had had sex. When I responded, "Yesterday," he slapped me and said, "You can't have venereal disease one day later; it takes at least a week for an infection to occur." The pain immediately disappeared. I realized then that the pain was my subconscious punishing me for having broken my superego taboo against sex. It also made me aware of the long road I had to travel before I could accept my body and its sexuality in a healthy way. Except for one experience of mutual masturbation with a distant relative, I had no sex with another person for the next fifteen years. The pain, shame, and guilt far outweighed any pleasure I experienced. With the exception of an occasional slip into masturbation, I managed to live out my commitment to celibacy.

On November 9, 1945, I was honorably discharged from the U.S. Army. I decided to return to Buffalo and complete the bachelor's program in fine arts at Canisius College I had begun before the war. I was aware that I was not fulfilling the promise I made to God in prison camp to join the Jesuits. I was also aware that a large part of my motivation at that point for entering religious life was survivor's guilt. Why was I allowed to return home alive, when so many of my friends and buddies were dead and buried in Europe? In fact, the first time I was back in Europe for graduate studies after my ordination, I traveled to the American War Cemetery in Alsace-Lorraine, where many of my friends from the 347th Regiment who died in battle were buried. I remembered them and all the dead American soldiers buried there in my mass and prayers. Later, I traveled to the American War Cemetery in Luxembourg and did the same. I was struck by the solitary grave of "Blood and Guts" Patton in front of thousands of graves of dead GIs. I remembered how we infantrymen used to joke about "*our* blood and *his* guts" and wondered what sort of reception he would get at the resurrection.

5

Vocation

I was still ambivalent about my vocation, which was still based primarily in my fear that as a gay man the only way I could get to heaven was by denying and suppressing my sexuality and my desire for human love and my belief that the only way to accomplish that denial was to enter a religious order, which would provide the environment and the support for a life of celibacy that was possible and meaningful. I decided to test my vocation by completing my undergraduate education at Canisius College.

During the next few years, 1945 to 1948, at Canisius, I threw myself into studies and extracurricular activities. I knew that whatever my vocation would be would include standing up and speaking in public, without paralyzing anxiety. In fourth grade, when I first had to speak in front of the class, my knees knocked together, I wet my pants, and I couldn't manage to say a word. To this day, I always go to the toilet before I get up to speak. At Canisius, I forced myself to take part in every activity that made me speak before an audience. I joined the college debate team, took part in oratory contests, sang in the glee club, and accepted roles in the college theater. I also became editor of the college newspaper. Over those three years, I became a very successful public speaker. In fact, in 1948, I tied for first place as an orator at the national finals of college competitions at Indiana University, and the Canisius debate team of which I was a member tied the University of Chicago for first place. I discovered that, although I couldn't eliminate my anxiety, by controlling it and channeling the energy that came from it, I was able to become a very effective speaker.

I graduated magna cum laude in June 1948, and finally the time had come for a decision. I continued to feel ambivalent about entering religious life. I realize now that my relationship with God was still based primarily on fear. As soon as I had my first good meal after prisoner-of-war camp, my sexual appetite came back in full force as well. I wanted to live my life in full accord with gospel values; I had great admiration for my Jesuit teachers and their ideal of integrating faith and knowledge. However, I still felt that my failure to control my sexual desires made me unworthy to join their ranks. I tried to imagine myself in some other profession. My oratorical abilities made me think I would be a good lawyer, so I went to the law school and sat in on lectures. I also considered medical school. But God would not let go of me, and I knew that I would regret it the rest of my life if I did not enter religious life and give it my best.

And so, to Katie's great joy, I entered the Jesuit novitiate at St. Andrew on Hudson in August 1948. As I rode in the taxi from the railroad station in Poughkeepsie to St. Andrew's, I tossed my last pack of Camel cigarettes out the window. My withdrawal from the world in the novitiate was going to be done cold turkey. Jim Demske, who had entered the Jesuits a year before me from Canisius, was assigned to me as my "angel." In later years, Jim served as the beloved president of Canisius College for many years until his death from leukemia in 1994. He brought me to the dormitory, where I was stripped of my lay clothes, which I never saw again; I was clothed with the black coat, the distinctive uniform of a Jesuit novice. I was struck with how similar this first day was to my first day as a prisoner of war. I tried to console myself with the thought that at least I was here voluntarily as a prisoner of love and could leave any time I wished.

For the next two years, I threw myself into the round of prayer, studies, and work that made up the life of a Jesuit novice. We began with a thirty-day silent retreat, where I learned the Jesuit style of reflecting on the Gospels by imagining myself on the scene with Jesus. Out of that process came a deeper love and desire to be Jesus' companion in life. For the first ten years, living in a celibate atmosphere with daily prayer and penance did allow me to keep sexual temptations at bay. I especially remember the day the novice master introduced us to the instruments of penance, the lash and the *catena*. On certain weeknights, before going to bed, at a signal we were to lash our backs with a rope whip, and on certain days we were expected to wear around our upper thighs the *catena*, a band of wire with sharp spikes sticking out and penetrating our skin. These practices were meant to help us mortify the flesh and keep our sexual appetites under control. (Thank God, these psychologically damaging practices were done away with after Vatican II!)

My first few years were very happy. I felt that I was growing into a deeper intimacy with God. I was assigned to work in the gardens and to decorate the altar on feast days, both activities in full accord with my gay sensitivities. I discovered the incredible effect dried sheep blood had on the growth of my gladioli in the garden. I also discovered that I could put plain white hydrangeas on the altar the evening before Pentecost, add red coal tar dye to the water, and have them change overnight into flaming red flowers. *Ecco, miracolo!* ("Behold, a miracle!") I was admonished for that feat by the house canon lawyer, who pointed out that, according to canon law, nothing artificial was to be used on the altar.

After two years in the novitiate and a year of juniorate, studying the classics in Latin and Greek, I began my study of philosophy at Woodstock and later at Bellarmine College on the shores of Lake Champlain. I took to philosophy like a duck to water. My favorite teacher, Father Norris Clarke, named me *homo naturaliter metaphysicus* "a natural born philosopher." I buried myself in Aristotle, Plato, and Thomas Aquinas. I wrote esoteric articles for the philosophical journal on the question, Is the human essence individualized by matter, or does every human have an absolutely unique act of existence? I was all for the latter. Another article questioned whether beauty was a property of a creature's essence or existence. Again, I argued for existence, because God as the source of all beauty is the unique being whose essence is his existence. Still another defended Martin Buber's theory that there were absolutely unique moments in history that represent the creative inbreaking of the divine into human history. I realize now that I buried myself in left-brain activity to escape dealing with my feelings and emotions. Before I finished studies, I managed to garner seven academic degrees.

While I was studying philosophy, Edward Sponga, S.J., the rector, introduced me to the thought of Maurice Blondel, a French preexistentialist philosopher from the turn of the century. Blondel's primary contribution was *Philosophie de l'Action*, published in 1893, in which he reflected brilliantly on a text from scripture: *qui fecit veritatem, venit ad lucem* ("he or she who does the truth, comes to the light"; John 3:21). Action, Blondel argued, has a synthetic power that brings a kind of knowing that can never be attained by the intellect alone. Blondel's book was given over to exploring that kind of knowing. A devout man of faith and prayer, Blondel argued that freely chosen actions can unite our spirits with the divine spirit. "Anyone who loves knows God because God is love!" I found my vocation to the Jesuits beautifully summed up in this passage from Blondel:

> To equal himself and to be saved, man must go beyond himself. To consent to an invasion of all that stands for a life that is prior and a will that is superior to his, is his way of contributing to his own creation. To will all that we will in complete sincerity of heart is to place in us the being and action of God. No doubt it does cost something, since we do not perceive how profoundly this will is our own. But one must give all for the all. Life has a divine value, despite the weaknesses of pride and sensuality; humanity is generous enough to want to belong more completely to the one who exacts more of it,

I did not realize it at the time, but I was laying the theoretical basis for my own movement out of academia into political and social activism. True to Blondel's philosophy of action, at every subsequent stage of my life, I combined a life of theory with a life of action.

For regency, normally a three-year period of teaching that all Jesuits had to undergo between the study of philosophy and theology, I returned to Canisius High School in Buffalo. Because of my age, my period of teaching was reduced to two years, 1955 and 1956. I taught seniors Latin and Greek. My first classes were extremely difficult. I was filled with anxiety and fear but soon discovered that I had a natural gift for teaching. Part of my responsibility was to teach Virgil's beautiful *Aeneid* to the fourth-year Latin students. In that poem, Aeneas, after wandering with his crew for twenty years as they tried to return home, wound up shipwrecked on the shores of Africa. In an effort to restore the shipwrecked crew's morale, Aeneas gave a pep talk that contained the beautiful line: *Forsan et haec olim meminisse iuvabit* ("Perhaps even this when remembered will give pleasure"). I printed that line on the classroom blackboard and made it our motto for all the hard work of translating and memorizing the *Aeneid*. It also became my lifelong motto. I coached the high school debate team, which was extremely successful and won many honors. I also directed the sodality, a religious organization that developed spiritual life and encouraged vocation to the priesthood and religious life.

Together with the sodality, I began to put Blondel's philosophy of action into practice. We went to the inner-city hospitals and asked the nurses for a list of patients who never or seldom had visitors. My students then visited these patients weekly and brought them little gifts, like a few cigarettes or a chocolate bar.

One patient was a professor of history who had been paralyzed in an automobile accident. The student who visited him lit a cigarette and held it to his lips while the professor gave his best advice on college studies and on becoming a scholar. The relationship that resulted was ideal for both parties, and a strong bond of affection developed.

One time, an elderly patient called me in, kissed my hands, and spoke anxiously to me in Polish. I found a nurse who could translate and learned he wanted to go home, but he could not be released unless someone from his family signed him out. We located the address he gave us on Buffalo's east side, under a railroad trestle. We knocked on the front door, and the woman who answered told us that the woman we were looking for lived in a shed in the back. There we met a ninety-year-old woman who said all her winter clothes had been burned in a fire from her wood stove. Besides her bed the only object in the shed was a beautiful statue of the Infant of Prague. She thought her husband would be better off staying in the hospital. We obtained winter clothes for both husband and wife, took the wife to the hospital to sign him out, and brought them both back to their shed. Then we found a social worker who was able to find them better housing.

A farmer who had been hit by a car begged us to go to his farm to milk his cows. It had been several days since they were milked, and the cows would be suffering badly. We had our first experience at milking cows and then alerted a neighbor to take over until the farmer returned. At the end of my two years of regency, at least eight of my students entered the Society of Jesus as novices.

In 1956, I returned to Woodstock Seminary in Maryland to begin the four-year program in theology. Once again, I threw myself into studies. I had entered the society when I was twenty-four, after completing undergraduate work in college. I studied for another eleven years before I was ordained in 1959. We used to joke that the Jesuits considered ordination as a reward for a well-spent life.

Again seeking to put theory into action, I joined a teaching ministry at

Henryton, a segregated tubercular hospital for African Americans outside Baltimore. Every Saturday, I sought out anyone who wanted to be instructed in the Catholic faith. I soon found out that many of the patients could not receive the operation they needed for their cure because they had no one to donate blood for them. Anyone undergoing an operation needed to have up to six pints of blood donated and kept in reserve. Many patients had languished for years because they could not find the requisite donors. There was a great reluctance in the African American community to donate blood. I recruited as many blood donors as I could from among the students at Woodstock. Anyone who saw me coming knew what I was after. I became known as the Vampire Jesuit.

One of my students at the hospital was an eighty-year-old man who had worked in the steel mills of Baltimore. He told me he had had enough of "hand-clapping" religion. He wanted to be instructed and baptized as a Catholic. I gave him a catechism and Bible and visited with him for about an hour every Saturday. When I suggested he read something, he would put on spectacles and look at the book. One day I had the intuition that he could not read. When I questioned him about it, he became frightened and asked me, "Do you have to be able to read in order to enter heaven!" "Of course not," I replied. "In fact, it may be a help getting there not to be able to read." From that day on, whenever I quoted scripture or said something he liked, he would have me write it on a white card. Then all week long he went about the hospital giving the cards to those who could read and asking them to read the cards to him. As a result, I soon had more than ten people preparing for Baptism with me. When my elderly patient died shortly after his Baptism, I wanted to hold a funeral mass at the hospital. I held the service but without his body because someone in the morgue, knowing he had no family, sold the cadaver to a local hospital.

6

Ordination

Ordination to the priesthood arrived finally for me in June of 1959, when I was thirty-four. I was ordained by Cardinal Spellman at the Fordham University student chapel and celebrated my first mass the next day at a side altar. Katie and my father were both too ill to attend. My three brothers and their wives; my sister, Sister Sheila; my eighth-grade teacher, Sister Ernestine; Sam Weisberg; John Thornton; and a large group of other relatives and ex-army friends joined me on that occasion. The next week, I returned to Buffalo and celebrated mass at home for Katie and my father.

Ordination brought my relationship with God to a crisis. During the retreat before ordination, I felt like a hypocrite because I was still in the closet and had never acknowledged my homosexuality to anyone. I feared that if I admitted my orientation I would be denied ordination. As I prostrated myself in the ordination ceremony at Fordham, I was begging God in a sort of despair to forgive me.

In the weeks following ordination, instead of joy, I felt the worst depression of my life. The depression centered around reciting the holy office, groups of psalms and prayers, at that time still in Latin, that all priests were required under mortal sin to recite at certain hours every day. I found it difficult to understand the Latin. We were required to speak each word of the office, even when we recited it in private. I had the horrible realization that after decades of struggle with sexual temptations, I had now added seven occasions of possible mortal sin to my life every day until I died. I found it almost impossible to recite the office and felt incredibly depressed every time I picked up the book. I interpreted that depression as a sign that God was angry with me for going ahead with ordination.

Fortunately around that time, I met a priest friend of mine who told me a joke that was making the rounds in clerical circles in Washington, D.C.

Three priests who had recently died met each other in hell. Pete asked Joe, "Why are you here?"

"I guess I got what I deserved," Joe answered. "I stole the parish funds and ran off to Florida, where I lived like a playboy until I was killed in an automobile accident. I never repented what I did. And why are you here, Pete?"

"Well, I deserve to be here," Pete answered. "I kept a mistress and sneaked out every night to be with her. I died in her arms without repentance." Then both of them turned to Pat.

"But Pat! Why are you here? We always thought you were a model priest and a saint. You worked all your life in a poor inner-city parish, you ran a soup kitchen, you never took a day off, you gave the shirt off your back to the poor. You're the last person in the world we thought we would meet here in hell!"

"Well," Pat said, "I guess I deserve to be here. On the last night of my life, I worked late in the parish. When I got home, I was exhausted, so I skipped vespers. That night I died of a heart attack. Here I am for all eternity in hell!"

As soon as I heard that joke, I was given the grace to realize my only motive for reading the holy office was fear and that God did not want me to worship out of fear. "For you did not receive a spirit of slavery to fall back into fear, but you have received a spirit of adoption. When we cry, 'Abba! Father!' it is that very Spirit bearing witness with our spirit that we are children of God" (Rom. 8:15–16). I closed my breviary and put it on the shelf, never to open it again, at least not in a fearful sense of obligation before the god of fear. I resolved then and there never to place any action in relation to God that was based primarily on fear of punishment because such an action was actually blasphemous to God. I would take a chance on God—that God was a God of love and did not want any worship based primarily on fear. As soon as I made that decision, my depression lifted, and for the first time since ordination I felt peace and joy in my heart and a renewed desire to be in the service of a God of love as a Jesuit priest.

A year later in 1960, I was sent back to Europe for tertianship and doctorate studies in philosophy at Louvain University in Belgium. Once again I found myself leaving New York harbor on the passenger ship *Queen Elizabeth*. This time, however, it was the *Queen Elizabeth II*, and I had a bed in a private cabin and superb food. The first summer of my return I spent at the Alliance Française in Paris, doing my best to understand and speak French. Because my skills in that language were poor, I spent most of that summer isolated and lonely because of the language barrier. There is terrible frustration in thinking the thoughts of an adult and being able to express them only in the language of a young child.

During that summer, after nearly fifteen years of celibacy, I first acted out my homosexual needs in a compulsive and self-destructive way. I searched out sexual encounters in the public toilets of Paris. By the time I arrived at our tertianship in Ghent, I was totally demoralized by my lack of control over my sexual needs. Tertianship was built into Jesuit formation to be a third year of novitiate, a year of prayer, studies, and penance, and also the time for the second thirty-day retreat, based on the spiritual exercises of Saint Ignatius. We were expected to emerge from tertianship as fully formed Jesuits.

Just before going to Ghent for tertianship, I once again applied the Blondelian principle of always joining action with reflection. I contacted my close friend and fellow Jesuit, Tom Egan, who was serving as chaplain for a tank corps of the American army in Germany. Tom was an ideal army chaplain, friendly, outgoing, compassionate, and deeply spiritual. During my years in Europe, I replaced Tom several times a year while he made his annual retreat or took a needed vacation. His army base was in Bavaria, close to the iron curtain. Each Sunday I celebrated mass at two bases in Bavaria and then flew in a two-man helicopter to the border of Czechoslovakia and offered mass on the flat hood of a jeep at several of the guard posts close to the front line with the Soviet troops.

During these visits, I first became involved in a ministry to gay people. Many of the eighteen-year-old soldiers who served in the medical corps or as chaplains' assistants were closeted gay men. Finding me a sympathetic counselor, they told me of gay friends who had been dishonorably discharged. In almost every case, the young soldiers were approached by older noncommissioned officers, who solicited them to perform sexual acts. Frequently, to cover themselves, these noncommissioned officers denounced the soldiers and claimed that the younger men had made the approach seeking sexual contact. Almost inevitably, the military court accepted the sergeant's word for what happened. As a result, the young gay soldiers lived in an atmosphere of constant fear, aware that any denunciation of them, even untrue, would result in a dishonorable discharge that could ruin their whole lives. These stories made me intensely aware of the total powerlessness of young gay men in the army and their exposure to injustice with no hope of a fair hearing. This same climate of injustice and fear continues today under Clinton's "Don't ask! Don't tell!" policy.

During those visits, I became friends with a commanding officer who was a very devout Catholic. His parents had died in a car accident when he was a young boy, and he was raised by his uncle, a priest, in the parish priest house. Every time this officer led troops into combat in World War II and Korea, he promised God to recite certain prayers every day the rest of his life if the troops he commanded were spared in battle. As a result, he ended up after a long military career with more than an hour of prayers he felt obliged to recite every day in fulfillment of his vows. He had to awake very early every morning to recite his prayers. They were now beginning to interfere with his ability to perform his duty. I was able to persuade him to substitute a short prayer of gratitude to God in place of the hour-long list of prayers.

My thirty-day retreat was due to begin in Belgium at the end of one of the visits to the army post in Germany. Just as I was preparing to return, the employees of the public transportation system in Belgium went on strike. I called the tertian master, a former general of the Society, to try to postpone my return to Ghent until the end of the strike. He was adamant that I be there for the opening of the retreat or else I would have to repeat the tertianship in another year.

When I told the commanding officer, he arranged for a military plane to fly me into Brussels and obtained diplomatic clearance for the plane. As we crossed some mountains in Germany, however, the wings of the plane iced, and we were forced to make an emergency landing. I then managed to get on a German train that brought me to the border of Belgium, at Aachen. I hitched across the border into Liège in the middle of the night. On the streets of Liège, riot police were hiding in doorways to prevent the strikers from rioting. I managed to make my way to the Jesuit residence, where I stayed for the night.

The next morning, one of the Jesuits drove me to the main highway that crossed Belgium, and I began to hitchhike. Suddenly, a high-powered sports car zoomed by. When the driver spotted a priest hitchhiking at the side of the road, he slammed on the brakes and zoomed back to pick me up. The young man was a member of Belgian royalty. He had been educated at a Benedictine Abbey school in England, so he had a special respect for clergy. He was delighted to learn that I was an American priest and a Jesuit. He spoke highly of the wonderful education he received from the Benedictines. He entertained me with all sorts of anecdotes about his stay in England. He reminded me of a character from the novels of P. G. Wodehouse. He told me that he lived in a hundred-room mansion in Ostend, where he entertained many houseguests every weekend, and he invited me to come as a guest some weekend. He delivered me to the door of the monastery in Ghent just in time for the opening session of our thirty-day retreat.

Once again, I threw myself into that year of spiritual formation with the hope that I could regain the grace of living a life of chastity. The monastery where I stayed was a thirteenth-century Augustinian monastery. It was constantly cold and damp. It rained nearly every day for the entire year. The food was atrocious. All of us Americans ended up with liver problems. In a trip in November 1960 to vote for Kennedy for President at the U.S. Embassy in Antwerp, we sought out the only Italian restaurant in town. The proprietor told us that whenever the Jesuit General, Father Jansens, who was a native Belgian, was in town, he came there to eat.

And the tertian master to whom I confessed my sexual activity sent me to a psychiatrist, who gave me a series of injections to reduce my libido. But all they seemed to do was enhance it.

7

The Quest

Having completed tertianship in Ghent, I moved to Louvain to begin my doctoral studies in philosophy in the autumn of 1961. Louvain had an excellent reputation as a world center for Catholic philosophical scholarship. In my first year, I took eight different courses. Once again, I took to studies like a duck to water. We had several first-rate teachers. Each course ended with an oral examination, all of which took place within a week. For the most part, these exams were in French. I had no idea how well I had done. When the announcements were made of the grades, I did not hear my name and assumed I failed. But minutes later I found that my name, badly mispronounced, had been the first called out with the grade of *Grande Distinction*. My thesis subject, "The Philosophy of Action of Maurice Blondel," was accepted, and I was free to begin the research and writing for my doctorate.

I think the strain of that year at Louvain, following on tertianship, led to some degree of burnout. I attempted a summer of study of the German language in the town of Bad Aibling in Bavaria. Coming back to Germany as a student after having been a prisoner of war there was a good corrective experience for me. The people I met at Bad Aibling were warm and hospitable. I celebrated mass every morning in a small chapel off the town square. When the sacristan learned that I was a Jesuit, he was overjoyed. The chapel had been built by Jesuits before the suppression of the society by Pope Clement XIV in 1773 and was dedicated to the memory of the Jesuit saint, Stanislaus Koska. I was the first Jesuit priest to celebrate mass there in two hundred years.

When the feast of Saint Ignatius Loyola came around on July 31, the townspeople arranged a solemn high mass, complete with a full choir and orchestra performing a Mozart mass, and held a special, all-day festival. This warm, human encounter with the German people helped to heal some of the wounds still remaining from my prison camp experiences.

I found myself so exhausted at the end of that summer that I could not concentrate on philosophical readings. I went to the south of France and hired out as a day laborer for the grape harvest. The outdoor work restored me, and after a few months I returned to Paris to begin research on Blondel. As soon as I was able, I moved again to Paris and took up residence with the French Jesuits at 42 Rue de Grenelle.

While in Paris, I put the Blondelian principle to work again. In line with Jesuit directives for ministry, I sought out a group to whom no one was ministering and set up a ministry for them. The priest-workers in Paris recommended that I get involved with a group of young men who were the children of German soldiers and French mothers. These young men's identity cards identified them as *pupilles de état* in such a way that their German parentage was obvious. As a result, they could not obtain work permits and were forced to resort to crime to survive. Most of them had been raised in orphanages and had been so badly treated that they had no respect for any French authority, not even the clergy. My French priest friends thought that I, as an American, might be able to reach them.

I donned a beret, climbed onto my motor scooter, and ventured out to meet this group, who hung out in a bistro near the Place Pigalle, not far from the place in Paris where Ignatius and his followers took their first vows. Because their conversations were frequently monitored by French intelligence officers, these youths insisted that each of us have a nickname—Le Petit, Le Gros, and the like. I was given the name Le Canard "the duck" and a small, stuffed duckling that I was to carry with me as proof of my identity, which I still keep on my desk

My first contact was with a young man with a tragic story. He told me that he had just received from the French government his mother's remains in the mail. She had been buried in a special graveyard as a hero of the resistance. But when the government learned that she had had a German lover and bore him a son, they dug up her remains and sent them to her son. I arranged a decent Catholic burial for his mother.

Soon I was the confidant of a group of these half-German orphans who lived by their wits and shared a couple of rooms near Place Pigalle. One night one of them came to me at Rue de Grenelle in obvious fear. He told me that an Algerian had come to his room looking for him. The Algerian mistook his roommate for him and shot and killed him. The story behind this killing was a group of Algerians in Paris involved in a slavery and prostitution ring. When a girl from the countryside came to Paris, one of the Algerians seduced the girl, pretended to be her lover, and had her move in with him. After a few months, he told the girl that he was in trouble with the French police and had to return to Africa, but he had to make the trip secretly. He gave the girl a one-way ticket to a city in Algeria and told her to go to a bistro there and wait for him. The address he sent her to was a house of prostitution. His reward was the equivalent of three thousand dollars for each girl he delivered.

My friend and his companion had taken it on themselves to warn these girls what was about to happen. The Algerians were furious to lose their meal ticket and decided to silence the young men who were giving their profit-making scheme away. I sent the young man to a friend's house in the country, where he could hide out until the heat was off.

The primary need of this group was to get new identity cards that would not reveal their identity as the children of German soldiers so they could obtain employment. With the help of some priests in the country, I was able to obtain the identity cards of some young men who had died and provide my friends with false identities that allowed them to enter the mainstream of society. Out of gratitude, when I was staying at the Jesuit residence in Chantilly, a group of these young men showed up to visit and told me that they had brought as a gift a van full of Camembert cheeses that they had stolen in Les Halles. I persuaded them to return the cheese to Paris and let the police know where the van could be found.

A year later, a letter from one of these young men told me that he was in prison, serving a five-year sentence for theft. He asked me if I could visit him in a prison in the suburbs of Paris. I discovered that to visit, I had to get the permission of a judge. The judge was highly suspicious of my motives and asked me why I wanted to make this visit. I reminded him that I was a priest and my motive was the gospel imperative, "I was in prison and you visited me" (Matt. 25:36). I finally obtained permission.

On a hot summer day in June, I stood in a long line of wives and mothers, waiting for visiting hour. When I finally approached the window, I handed the guard my judicial permit and asked to see Monsieur Oberthal. The guard answered with great anger, "There are no 'monsieurs' here, there are only numbers! What number do you wish to see?" I realized there was a number next to my friend's name and read it to him. We were ushered into a great hall with small cells that looked like confessionals surrounding it. There was a wire grate between the prisoner and the visitor. The guards called out a prisoner's number and the letter of one of the cells. When my friend's number was called, I entered the designated cell. He was delighted to see me. I was his first visitor since he entered prison. He had asked me to come because his girlfriend had given birth to their first child. Because they were not legally married, she could not visit him with the child for the next five years of his imprisonment. He broke into tears and asked if I could arrange their marriage in prison so that she and his child could visit him. I contacted the prison chaplain, who seemed highly skeptical, but he promised to look into it.

Once I took up residence in Paris, my compulsive acting out of sexual needs took over once again with all the old shame, guilt, and self-hatred. It became much worse because all the prayers, penance, and petitions of tertianship seemed to have fallen on deaf ears. One night I found myself standing on the bank of the Seine. My despair had reached a climax, and I was ready to commit suicide by jumping into the river. Right at that time I experienced a special grace from God, a deep trust that God was hearing my prayers and was close to me even in my acting out. I felt God was sending me a message similar to the one he sent to St. Paul:

> Therefore, to keep me from being too elated, a thorn was given me in the flesh.
> . . . Three times I appealed to the Lord about this, that it would leave me, but
> he said to me, "My grace is sufficient for you, for power is made perfect in weakness." So, I will boast all the more gladly of my weaknesses, so that the power
> of Christ may dwell in me. (2 Cor. 12:7b–9)

God would not take away my "thorn in the flesh." God's grace would be sufficient for me, and that thorn would keep me humble. I was to carry on the struggle and not despair but trust that God was somehow allowing me to go through all this because there was a purpose in it. God in his wisdom would somehow bring good out of this. I did not know how, but I had to trust. I began to cry and felt a level of faith, hope, and trust I had never experienced before.

I recalled the words of the collect for the fifth Sunday in Lent: "Help us to embrace the world you have given us, that we may transform the darkness of its pain into the life and joy of Easter." I understood that God wanted me to experience all the pain and suffering of my gay brothers and lesbian sisters so that I could bring myself and them to the Easter joy of belief in God's love for us as gays. I was being called to be a "wounded healer."

Shortly after that incident, I moved to Aix-en-Provence. Maurice Blondel had spent the last years of his life as a professor at the University of Aix, during which time he became blind. One of his students, Natalie Panis, left her convent and became his secretary, and for eighteen years she served as his hands and his eyes. She read to him every day and wrote down the work he dictated. After Blondel died, his apartment in Aix was left unchanged, and Natalie Panis was left in charge of Blondel's archives. I visited Blondel's son, who was a *conseil d'état*, a federal supreme court judge, and received permission to work in the archives. Natalie Panis was very welcoming and helped me locate all the documents I needed for my thesis. She wrote in the preface to my publication, *The Blondelian Synthesis*, "I recall telling you that you seemed quite naturally to have parachuted down, as it were, into the very center of that difficult philosophy, but a philosophy whose inexhaustible riches and fecundity you have already intuited in your previous studies."

A year later in 1963, carrying a heavy suitcase, I set out from my residence in Aix to go to Germany once again to assist Tom Egan. Along the road to the train station, I inadvertently stepped off into a ditch. I was taken to the hospital in Aix with a broken leg. The doctors in the local hospital put my leg in an emergency cast and sent me to American Hospital in Paris. The doctors thought I would receive much better treatment there because American Hospital had an excellent reputation. It was founded by an American woman whose son died in France because of inadequate medical attention. I was taken by ambulance to the train from Aix to Paris. An ambulance met the train in Paris and took me to the hospital.

The American doctor in the emergency room, a graduate of the Jesuit Boston College, seemed excited when he learned that I was a Jesuit. He made sure that I was assigned to a specific room. I found out later that my roommate was an elderly member of parliament whose home was in the south of France. His claim to fame was that after World War I he tried to pass a bill that called for the expulsion of all Jesuits from France, despite the fact that most of them had served in the French army. The doctors wanted him to leave the hospital and return to his home. He did not wish to leave, however, because his mistress lived in Paris. When she visited, she was very affectionate, kissing and hugging him, whereas when his wife visited she was cold and all business. During visiting hours, the room was full with many of my Jesuit friends from Paris. We roommates got along well and, as I left for my operation, he tried to reassure me, but a day later he left the hospital.

After I had returned to Aix, I was confined to bed for several weeks, but, because of Natalie Panis, I was able to continue my work on my thesis. Kind and solicitous, she came to my room in the priests' residence with a basket of fresh fruit and a file of Blondel's writings and letters she knew would be useful to me for my thesis.

Little did I realize then how I was to recapitulate Blondel's problems with the Vatican because of his writings. His primary book, *Philosophy of Action*, challenged the integration of Catholic thought with Thomistic objective realism and claimed that a better integration could be made between modern subjectivism and Catholic theology. Garigou LaGrange and other powerful voices in the Vatican immediately attacked Blondel and successfully sought to have his work condemned. Blondel had a defender in Cardinal Martini, later to become Pope Pius XII. The final word Blondel received from the Congregation for the Defense of the Faith was that his book would not be condemned, but only on condition that he never publish again in his lifetime. Blondel obeyed that order and left five major volumes of work to be published posthumously. This attack on the subjectivism of Blondel's thought was recently renewed with the publication of *Splendor Veritatis* by Pope John Paul II. Garigou LaGrange had been the pope's teacher.

I spent two years in Aix-en-Provence immersed again in Blondel's thought. He produced the most effective integration of Christian faith and modern philosophy, but the Vatican has successfully blocked any recognition of his achievement. When I was studying theology, the only mention of his name occurred in footnotes as an adversary of classical theological teaching based in Thomistic objective realism.

8

Discovering Gay Love

In those years I made another major step in my spiritual journey toward accepting my gayness as God's gift. One weekend, I took a break from my studies and took a trip to the city of Avignon in the south of France. While I was visiting the papal palace there, I met someone in the papal gardens to whom I found myself powerfully attracted. It was Tony Jonesco, a man a few years younger than I, who was to become my first gay lover. A burly man with a big black mustache, he had the classic physique of a French peasant. During our long conversation in the gardens, he was very kind and gracious. He invited me to come and visit with him in his home in Valliguere, a village near the Pont du Gar, about fifteen miles from Avignon.

Very quickly we developed a strong bond of affection and friendship. Tony was the only child of wealthy parents and had lived in a chateau in the south of France. His mother was a member of the royal family of Provence; his father, from Romania, was a flyer with the Escadrille Lafayette who had died in an airplane crash while Tony was a child. His mother then remarried a wealthy Englishman who was Jewish.

Tony had had a privileged childhood. He had studied to be a concert pianist with some of the most famous teachers in Paris. We spent many a sunny afternoon together in Valliguere as he performed classical concerts with great skill and love. He once brought me to a party in Paris given by the Aly Khan, who had been his classmate in school. When the Aly Khan learned that I was a Jesuit priest, he took me aside and discussed with me his attraction to the Catholic faith, which he attributed to his French mother. I suggested that he seek an audience with the pope. I, in turn, talked about my half-German war orphans, many of whom had worked in his stables while they were in the orphanage.

When the news came that World War II was coming to an end, Tony had hurried home from his school in Lyons to share the joy with his family. He discovered the bodies of his mother and stepfather murdered in their bedroom. One of the last acts of the departing Nazis was to murder them and loot the chateau. His parents had sold all their possessions at the beginning of the war in the hope of escaping to England. The entire family fortune had been stolen. The only person Tony found still alive was his English nanny, Missy, a woman in her seventies. With no money to pay taxes and utilities, Tony had been forced to sell the chateau and move into a farmhouse in Valliguere with Missy, some antique furniture, and a magnificent grand piano. For many years, Tony was unable to recover from the tragedy. He stayed at home practicing on his piano and composing essays and stories that he hoped someday to publish. He survived by selling, piece by piece, the antique furniture he rescued from the chateau. When I met him, he was down to the last few pieces.

Tony lived in poverty; the farmhouse he rented had no electricity or running water or toilet. When darkness fell, we lit a candle to eat and read by. Tony often said, "One candle is misery, but two candles are a luxury!" One of my first nights there, I had to use the bedpan. I offered to carry it down to a stream and empty it out. To do so, I had to cross the village square, where all the women of the village were washing their laundry, and then cross the road to get to the stream. Tony told me to wait until noon when all the women would be home cooking lunch. I kept asking, "Is it time yet?" Tony looked out and replied, "Not yet!" Finally, he gave his OK. I set out with the bedpan in a brown paper bag. Just as I arrived at the highway, a police car was passing by. In 1962, the Algerian war was still going on, and the police were suspicious of any strangers. They jumped out of their patrol car, surrounded me with drawn guns, and demanded to know who I was and what I had in the bag! Luckily, I had a visa in my passport written in French that allowed me to reside as a student in Belgium. They assumed that because the visa was written in French, it was a permit to be in France. Then to my great embarrassment—and theirs—they demanded that I show them what I had hidden in the paper bag. They quietly handed it back, got in their car, and quickly drove off.

Every chance I had over the next two years, I visited Tony in Valliguere. From his home we could see the famous Roman aqueduct, Pont du Gar, and in summer we went swimming in the Gar. Tony, in turn, visited me in Aix and later in Paris. The bond of affection between us grew ever deeper. The real-ization dawned on me that the drive in me that underlay my compulsive act-ing out was a drive toward intimacy. The sexual acting out was based in a despair of ever achieving sexual intimacy in the context of human love. In the Genesis 2 account of creation, the oldest in the Old Testament, God says: "It is not good that any human be alone; every human needs a companion of his or her own kind!" (This translation is recommended by the biblical scholar, Phyllis Trible.) In the companionship Tony and I achieved, I felt a peace and joy I had never experienced before. In our mutual love, I began to believe for the first time that I was lovable and capable of giving a healthy and holy love in a homosexual context. In turn, I had greater faith and trust in God's love for me. "Beloved, let us love one another, because love is from God; everyone who loves is born of God and knows God. Whoever does not love does not know God, for God is love" (1 John 4:7–8).

With God's grace, our relationship proved of mutual help. Tony's love helped me to restore my faith and trust in God's love. I, in turn, was able to be a great help to Tony in recovering his family fortune. Following the war, the Germans agreed to make reparations to anyone whose property had been stolen because of anti-Semitism. A committee was set up in the Jewish community to deter-mine who deserved recompense. Tony had filled out the requisite forms several times, only to be told that they had been misplaced or lost. He had despaired of ever achieving justice in this matter and was convinced that the fact that he personally was not Jewish was the reason his case could not get a fair hearing. When I returned to Paris, I sought and obtained an interview with the chief rabbi in Paris, who was in charge of the reparations process, to plead Tony's cause. I presented his case successfully, and shortly after I left Europe, Tony re-ceived the reparations he had been seeking for two decades.

Meeting Tony was one of the greatest blessings God has sent into my life. From that point on, I began the positive process of accepting my gayness as God's gift and a special blessing. I still had a long way to go, but the journey was off to a good start. My relationship with Tony freed me to give all my psy-chic energy over to completing my thesis on Maurice Blondel. The manuscript was ready for defense by the summer of 1964: "The Blondelian Synthesis: A Study of the Influence of German Philosophical Sources on the Formation of Blondel's Method and Thought."

Tony came with me to Louvain and helped me prepare my doctoral defense in impeccable French. The defense was a major ordeal. I was questioned by teachers speaking English, French, and German, and I had to answer in the language the question was asked. When the jury returned to the room, they announced that I had earned my doctorate with the honor of *Plus Grande Distinction*, the highest honor that Louvain had to give.

I found out later that, through my research in Aix, Louvain University became aware of a treasure trove of unpublished manuscripts and letters in Blondel's former apartment at Aix. They were afraid that I might purchase this resource for Fordham. Secretly, behind my back, they negotiated with the Blondel family to have the Blondelian archives relocated to the University of Louvain library.

Immediately following the award of the degree, the monsignor who was head of the philosophy department invited me to his private quarters. I assumed I was being invited to a celebration of my success. To my chagrin, I was handed an oath of fidelity to Rome's teachings and ordered to take that oath on an open Bible. This left a bad taste after what had been a very joyous day. I was never able to understand the oath-taking mentality, except to see it based in distrust and paranoia. Although the oath was probably required of all doctorate students, I suspect that I was under extra suspicion as to my orthodoxy because my thesis was on the thought of Maurice Blondel, whom the church distrusted. Even had I seen what was coming, I'm not sure what else I would have done.

A few days later, Tony and I tearfully said goodbye. Parting from him was one of the most painful experiences of my life. We had sporadic contact by mail over the next few years. Later, I learned that Tony had married and was living in Lyons. A few years ago, I managed to find a telephone number for a Mrs. Tony Jonesco in a telephone directory for Lyons. Mrs. Jonesco told me that Tony had died, and I experienced again the grief I felt when we parted in Belgium.

9

Triumphant Return?

I returned to the United States aboard one of the Holland-American liners in June 1964. As soon as I boarded in Antwerp, I saw an announcement that Heiko Oberman, at that time on the faculty of Harvard Divinity School, was to give a talk that evening. He had been one of the Protestant observers at the first session of Vatican II and was reporting on his experience. I went to the lecture, eager to learn what was happening in Rome. To my dismay, the lecture was delivered in Dutch. After the lecture, I introduced myself. When he learned that I had just completed a doctoral study on Maurice Blondel, he became very excited. He told me that the name of Maurice Blondel came up frequently in the council debates and that he knew very little about him. He asked to borrow my manuscript and read it while we were on our way to America. Two days later, he returned the manuscript. He told me he found it excellent and would like to submit it as the first volume in a new series he was editing, Studies in the History of Christian Thought, to be published by Brill in Leiden. It was, in fact, published in 1966. The board of editors of the series sounded like a who's who of the academic world: Henry Chadwick of Oxford, Edward Dowey of Princeton, Jaroslav Pelikan of Yale, and Brian Tierney of Cornell.

I could not believe my good luck and felt gratitude to God. At the time, my self-image was that I would become a famous teacher of philosophy at one of the Jesuit graduate schools, dressed in gabardine and smoking my pipe. In fact, in the next few years, I did produce a series of scholarly papers on Blondel's thought, which I delivered at various philosophical conventions. In 1968, I wrote a commentary on Blondel, "Necessary Structures of Freedom," published in the *Proceedings of the Jesuit Philosophical Association*, an attempt to prove that subjective freedom did not necessarily imply situational relativism and the absence of all norms. This charge against my position has been made in recent dialogue by critics of my belief that gay sex can be morally justified in the context of gay love.

In 1969, I produced another article, "The Relation between Philosophy and Religion in Blondel's Thought," published in the *Proceedings of the American Catholic Philosophical Association*. I then published "Freedom and the Future," applying Blondel's thought to genetics, in *Theological Studies*, September 1972, and "Blondel on the Subjectivity of Moral Decision Making" in the 1974 *Proceedings of the American Catholic Philosophical Association*. Blondel's thinking on this topic of the subjectivity of moral decision making is in direct contradiction to the thinking of Pope John Paul II in his encyclical *Splendor Veritatis*. In the summer of 1966, I was invited to teach a course on Blondel at the Fordham University graduate school in philosophy. I thought I had arrived academically, but I was soon to be disillusioned.

When my book was published by Brill in 1966, it received a great deal of publicity in Europe. One whole issue of a philosophical publication at the University of Genoa was given over to critical discussion of it. But the book was never critically reviewed in any philosophical publication in America, and I was never again invited to teach a course on Blondel. My book and all those articles seemed to drop into some sort of black hole in the philosophical universe.

My Jesuit superiors assigned me to teach undergraduate courses at LeMoyne College in Syracuse, New York. My teaching was confined to introductory courses in the history of philosophy and a course for seniors in Christian ethics. I arrived at LeMoyne just as the turmoil over the war in Vietnam was at its height. Because I taught a course in Christian ethics, I was obliged to deal with the "just war" issue. I became convinced that our participation in the war in Vietnam did not qualify as a just war. Therefore, anyone who was a sincere Christian had a moral obligation to be a conscientious objector. Following the Blondelian principle of "doing the truth," I became very active in the antiwar movement by addressing student rallies and sit-ins directed against the war. I was very much influenced by my Jesuit colleague and friend, Daniel Berrigan, who had left LeMoyne the year before I got there.

On one occasion, I traveled to Utica, New York, with a Jesuit scholastic,

Jim Bernauer, to take part in an antiwar demonstration. There were only a few hundred of us in the antiwar parade, but several thousand protested our presence. When the parade ended, I gave an impassioned talk at the Unitarian Church in downtown Utica on the immorality of the war and the obligation of followers of Christ to be conscientious objectors. A riot broke out, and the local police escorted Jim and me out of town. We were ordered never again to put foot in Utica or we would be immediately arrested for disturbing the peace. Recently Jim, who is now a professor of philosophy at Boston College, assured me that he has never since set foot in Utica.

As a result of my high profile in the antiwar movement in Syracuse, a group of Democrats asked if I would run for the U.S. Congress as a "dove" candidate in a primary against the "hawk" incumbent, Jim Hanley. I was very aware that my homosexuality, if it became public, would be a serious handicap for me. When I told my provincial, Father Jim Mitchell, about the invitation during his visitation to LeMoyne, he strongly recommended that I not accept the invitation. He told me that Father Robert Drinan was about to run for Congress in Boston and that two Jesuits running at the same time would look like a conspiracy. I then asked him, "What if I decide to run after all?" I liked his answer: "Well, let me know, and we'll discuss it further." I prayed over the invitation and came to the decision through a process of prayerful discernment that this was not God's will for me.

My antiwar activity made me very unpopular with the Jesuit community at LeMoyne, who, for the most part, were very conservative men. To my knowledge, none of them had read my book, *The Blondelian Synthesis*, or ever discussed it with me. In addition, I was one of the first to ask the superior for permission to wear civilian clothing, rather than the Roman collar, in the classroom. I thought it was inappropriate to wear a symbol of authority, implying that I had all the answers, in a course that purported to be a free and autonomous inquiry into philosophical questions. The superior, Father Andrew Brady, granted me permission and announced to the community that if anyone had any questions I would be glad to answer them. After the community meeting, one of the older priests approached me and said, "Father Brady told me that if I asked you, you would tell me why you are ashamed of your priesthood!" I responded that since he had already decided on the answer, why ask the question?

The hostility toward me in the community grew. Whenever I entered the common rooms, conversation stopped, and the priests got up and walked out. One day an elderly priest, a founder after whom a building was named, while "in his cups," accosted me and told me, "If they ever named you superior of this house, I would leave the Jesuits!" I moved out of the Jesuit residence and lived in one of the dormitories as a student counselor and stopped taking part in the Jesuit community activities. I learned years later that when the news arrived at LeMoyne that I had been dismissed from the Jesuits by the General, a group of the Jesuits broke out a bottle of champagne to celebrate.

I enjoyed teaching and counseling the undergraduates. I became a popular teacher, and a bond of affection formed between me and the students. Several of those friendships have lasted to this day. While in Buffalo to attend a basketball game, a group of my students spotted Freddie's Donut Shop on Main Street. They had heard my story about dreaming of eating dozens of Freddie's doughnuts while I was in prison camp. They bought three dozen doughnuts and left them at my door in the dormitory.

Once again, I tried to bury myself in my work and repress my need for sexual companionship, and once again it did not work. My loneliness and sense of isolation became intolerable. When I took vows as a Jesuit, I committed myself sincerely to attempt to live my entire life as a celibate priest and religious. The first fifteen years of my life as a Jesuit, I did succeed, with God's grace and intense prayer and self-discipline, to live out my commitment to a life of celibacy. But celibacy never came easy for me. Every day was a struggle to control my sexual fantasies and desires. I always understood that the grace of celibacy was a special gift that God gave to certain people. I have known many religious priests and other religious who received this grace. As a result, they were able to live out happy and healthy celibate lives. Their celibacy in no way interfered with their ability to form warm and affectionate intimate relationships.

I am also aware of many priests, religious, and laymen whose celibacy is grounded in pathology, fear of the body, fear of sexuality, and, most important, fear of human intimacy. In my psychotherapy practice over the years, I became aware that many priests and religious, both gay and straight, are called to ministry but not called to celibacy. They bring the message of God's love to thousands, but they are aware that a necessary condition for their ministry is their own personal involvement in a relation of intimate sexual human love and companionship. In an exhortation to one of the first communities of celibate religious, St. Augustine pointed out that the foolish virgins without oil in their lamps were indeed chaste, but their chastity was without love. They were incapable of a warm, loving response to the human needs of others and as a result were excluded from the kingdom of God, which is a kingdom of love. Sexual abstinence can be of a type that tends to be morally evil and psychologically destructive.

Discernment of my own experience led me to the conclusion, after many years of struggle, that God was calling me to a ministry to gay and lesbian people but was not calling me to a life of celibacy. Because of my positive experience with Tony in France, an experience of deep peace and joy, which transformed my relationship with God from one of fear to one of love, I made the decision to seek out a gay friendship. My hope was that all my psychic energy, caught up in a struggle to suppress sexual needs, would be freed and made available for loving ministry.

10

Search and Discovery

Several weekends in 1964 and 1965, during the time I was teaching philosophy and was student counselor at LeMoyne College in Syracuse, I went to New York City to try to meet someone at the gay bars. The gay scene in New York at that time was treacherous. Most bars had notices in their windows that they were under police surveillance. And because homosexuality was considered criminal, predators were on the loose, circling like sharks. Many pretended to be gay and picked up gay patrons, usually out-of-towners. Once they were behind the closed doors of the visitor's hotel room, the "shark" attacked and robbed his gay victim, frequently at knifepoint or with a gun, sometimes injuring him, in some cases fatally, or the shark began a process of blackmail, threatening to tell the man's wife or boss or bishop. In three visits to New York, I was mugged three times. So the realization dawned on me that I was a poor judge of character, too naive for the sophisticated New York gay scene, or both.

Needless to say, my old feelings of self-hatred, shame, and guilt began to run riot again. At the same time, I observed how the atmosphere of homophobia fostered by church and state allowed gay people to be victimized without recourse of any kind. According to the pastoral practice of the Catholic church, if a man got drunk and went to a gay bath and had sex Saturday night, he could go to confession on Sunday morning and be absolved. But if he met someone and fell in love and they moved in together, he should be denied absolution until he broke up the relationship. Ironically, the church fostered promiscuity and felt that the enemy was not gay sex but gay love. Even the police were involved in the insidious practice of entrapment, soliciting gay men and then arresting them when they responded.

I prayed to God for the grace someday to be able to eliminate the atmosphere of despair and hatred. In one of the collects of Lent is the prayer: "Help us to embrace the world you have given us, that we may transform the darkness of its pain into the life and joy of Easter." The world God had led me into was the gay world and I saw that God's will for me was to do what I could with God's grace to fulfill that prayer.

Before I gave up my search entirely in despair, I decided to try another city where I'd heard there was a substantial gay presence; my next trip was to Canada, to the city of Toronto. I found the gay scene there much more laid-back and friendly. On my second trip, during New Year's weekend of 1965–1966, I went to the St. Charles Bar to join someone I'd met the day before, who had both an alcohol problem and an ulcer problem. He was drinking his whiskey in a glass of milk in the mistaken reasoning that the mixture would not aggravate the ulcer. In the course of the evening, a friend he had been hoping to meet there came up behind us at the bar. At first I was hostile, thinking that my companion would leave me for this younger man. But that younger man was Charles Chiarelli, thirty years old, ten years my junior, and as it turned out, he was immediately attracted to me and I to him. He quickly made his move, and that night I found myself going home with him to his apartment in the suburbs. Charlie and I have been lovers from that 1965 New Year's Eve until this day.

Charlie has a handsome Italian appearance. He is also a very warm and compassionate person. He has a marvelous sense of humor and is one of the most unselfish and generous people I know. He is a deeply spiritual person with a passion for justice and a deep concern for all the children in the world who suffer. Above all, once he makes a commitment, he loves passionately and faithfully unto death.

Charlie's father and mother were immigrants from Sicily. They ran a fresh fruit and vegetable store in Hamilton, Ontario. On my second visit to Toronto, Charlie brought me to Hamilton and introduced me to his family. They accepted me as Charlie's friend and eventually as a member of the family. Over the years, I presided at the funeral of Charlie's grandmother and father and celebrated the marriages of two of his nieces.

For the next six months, I traveled to Toronto when I had a free weekend, or Charlie flew or drove down to Syracuse. During that time, Charlie was sent by his employer to St. Louis on an assignment for a few weeks. When he mentioned to me on the phone that he was cruising around and discovering a lot of interesting bars, I flew there immediately to establish my "claim." That weekend really bonded us to each other, and our relationship became a commitment. Shortly after he returned to Toronto, he found a job as an electrical engineer at General Electric in Syracuse and moved there to start our life together.

For a couple of weeks, Charlie stayed at a motel while he searched for an apartment. The first weekend he was there, I was rushed to the hospital when I had a severe reaction to some oral penicillin I took for a sinus infection. As I regained consciousness in the emergency room, I heard the doctor say urgently, "Get a priest and have this man anointed immediately!" His words gave me a real scare. Until then, I had been fairly calm. I pleaded with God to let me live long enough to complete the footnotes for my book on Blondel and develop my friendship with Charlie. I was released from the hospital the next day.

During one of the first weekends we spent together after he moved into an apartment, Charlie was cooking up breakfast while I was sitting at the table. At one point, he quietly came up behind me and suddenly started pouring wheat germ over my head from a jar he was holding in his hand. There I was, with wheat germ granules in my hair, down my collar, on my chest and lap. At first I thought, Oh! Oh! I knew this was too good to be true! This guy's some sort of kook! What did I get involved with? I looked up and demanded, "What the hell is this all about? Why are you doing that?"

"Well, I had to do it!" Charlie exclaimed.

"What do you mean you had to? Why?"

"Well," he answered, "it says right here on the bottle, 'Pour this over your favorite *fruit*.'" It was then that I was certain I loved him. Charlie's incredible sense of humor has kept us both grounded for more than three decades. For the first fifteen years of our relationship, Charlie handled all our expenses since the only money I had to spend was a ten-dollar-a-week allowance from the Jesuits.

Secure in Charlie's love, I grew every day in my sense of gratitude to God and in my realization that God was giving me the grace to accept my own homosexuality so that I could help others. I prayed continuously that God would grant me the grace to see what God wanted of me and the courage to do it. I was well aware that the moment I began to write and speak about homosexuality, I myself would be under suspicion, and before long my relationship with Charlie could become public. I might have had to make a choice between my relationship with Charlie and my priesthood and membership in the Jesuits, which I valued very highly. The deep peace and joy I experienced in the exercise of my priesthood led me to believe that God wanted me to continue on as long as I could in the priesthood and the Jesuits. Yet I hated the hypocrisy of pretending to lead a celibate life and prayed continually for a way out of that dilemma. Paradoxically, that tension came to an end, much later, the day the Jesuits, under orders from the Vatican, expelled me from the order.

11

Extracting the Truth

While I was teaching at LeMoyne College, John Milhaven, a fellow Jesuit and professor of moral theology at Woodstock Seminary, published "Homosexuality and the Christian" in the May 1968 issue of *Homiletic and Pastoral Review* on the morality of homosexuality. Milhaven argued that modern morality, "relying exclusively on communal experience which in this case is preeminently the findings of psychology and psychiatry," ends up condemning homosexuality as immoral even more vehemently than traditional morality did. As soon as I read this article, I immediately felt called by God to bring all my talents for analysis and writing to bear on the issue of homosexuality. I recognized immediately that Milhaven was writing from the viewpoint of an outsider, a heterosexual who could understand homosexuality only as a spectator from without, and that he had no way to evaluate the materials he was dealing with from personal experience. The realization dawned on me that no one could write authentically about the ethics and morality of homosexuality who did not experience it from within him or herself. Just as no man can effectively undertake feminist studies, so no straight is in the position to undertake gay studies effectively. In fact, a short while after writing his article on homosexuality, John Milhaven left the Jesuit order to marry. I replaced him on the Jesuit faculty at Woodstock Seminary as professor of Christian ethics.

Milhaven attempted to argue on the basis of psychological "evidence" that homosexuality is a mental disease and that all homosexual relationships are necessarily destructive of both parties and, therefore, ultimately immoral. Milhaven agreed that all "Christians who live by the new morality base all their moral judgments and their lives on something positive though general: the absolute divine command to love." Facing the question of homosexual behavior, they would say, "God has laid down no specific and absolute prohibition of homosexual behavior. But He and I want absolutely one thing: that I live a life of love."

Love, Milhaven argued, is not just a question of feeling; experience teaches the honest person that some affectionate impulses lead to actions that, in the long run, hurt very badly the person he or she loves. Love, then, must be understood as "the free determination, commitment of a man or woman to further the good of a certain person." Milhaven admits that this is an old principle:

> Its newness has to do with an exclusive reliance on experience rather than *a priori* laws. However, since any one individual's experience of homosexuality is extremely limited, we must turn to the experience of the community, we must turn to those who have extensive critical experience, preeminently the psychologists, psychiatrists and analysts.

Milhaven drew the following conclusion:

> A man having genuine love for himself and others will refrain in his behavior from expressing and deepening particular feelings when the evidence on hand indicates strongly, if not with absolute certainty, that the feelings are profoundly immature and disordered. Consequently, a Christian moving in the spirit of the new morality condemns homosexual behavior more severely than one using traditional arguments. . . . According to the Christian, moved only by love, relying on the experience of the community, homosexual behavior is wrong in that it frustrates the man himself. It fixates him at a stage far short of the full emotional and sexual development of the "being man" who is God's glory.

I knew immediately on reading this article that it was totally wrong. My own personal experience of gay love both with Tony in Europe and with Charlie here at home was joyous and fulfilling. Contrary to being "profoundly immature and disordered," these relationships had helped me and my lovers to grow in maturity and health. I decided then to begin research on this subject and look into the so-called empirical evidence from the psychologists and psychiatrists that Milhaven relied on.

One school of psychiatrists, I found, did maintain that homosexuality, in all cases, represented a mental illness. Edmund Bergler, in *Homosexuality: Disease or Way of Life* (New York: Colliers, 1956), defines *homosexuality* as "a neurotic distortion of the whole personality. . . . There are no healthy homosexuals. The entire personality structure of the homosexual is pervaded by the unconscious will to suffer. This wish is gratified by self-created trouble-making (psychic masochism). . . he is an emotionally sick person." It is immediately evident in reading these authors that their judgment has nothing to do with empirical evidence. Rather, it is based on an ideological a priori judgment. Irving Bieber, for example, in *Homosexuality: A Psychoanalytic Study* (New York: Basic Books, 1962), writes, "We assume that heterosexuality is the biologic norm, and that unless interfered with all individuals are heterosexual. . . . All psychoanalytic theories assume that adult homosexuality is psychopathological and assign different weights to constitutional and experiential components."

In contrast to these homophobic psychiatrists, another school dealt with homosexuality as a healthy variation in human sexual orientation. For example, Wainwright Churchill, in *Homosexual Behavior among Males* (New York: Hawthorn Books, 1967), wrote, "This author wishes to go on record as one clinician among a multitude of others who has had the opportunity to interview and, in several cases, to have become acquainted with homosexual males who meet with every reasonable standard of mental health in their relationship with themselves and with others." New studies were beginning to emerge of individuals who live relatively discreet, stable, law-abiding, constructive, and socially useful lives as homosexuals. This group constitutes the largest proportion of those engaging in homosexual practices. The most important study done at that time in America on the "well-adjusted homosexual" was that of Evelyn Hooker published in the New York Council of Churches report, *Foundations for Christian Family Policy* (1961). Hooker sought out as her research subjects those homosexuals "who did not seek psychiatric help and who led relatively stable, occupationally successful lives." When the results of these tests were compared to those of tests administered to a like group of heterosexuals, psychologists found great difficulty in determining who were the homosexuals and in many cases "no evidence of any demonstrable pathology." Michael Shofield, in a similar comparative study conducted in England, *Sociological Aspects of Homosexuality*, supported Hooker's conclusions.

Fortunately, there seemed to be a growing awareness of the false scientific pretensions as well as the antihuman and immoral attitude of some psychologists and psychiatrists. Thomas Szasz, for example, in *The Manufacture of Madness* (New York: Harper, 1970), writes about the "great ideological conversion from theology to science," which redefined sin as sickness and moral sanction as medical treatment. "This change from a religious and moral to a social and medical conceptualization and control of personal conduct affects the entire discipline of psychiatry and allied fields. Perhaps nowhere is the transformation more evident than in the modern perspective on so-called sexual deviations, and especially on homosexuality."

Szasz accused his fellow psychiatrists of involving themselves in a program of social control that has nothing to do with genuine scientific medicine. They arrive at this position, he states, by pretending that social conventions are identical with nature, and by confusing the question of disobeying a traditional personal prohibition with mental illness:

> They establish themselves as agents of social control and at the same time disguise their primitive interventions in the semantics and social trappings of medical practice. Clearly, the question the psychiatrist is posing when he speaks of homosexuality as illness concerns not the traditional concept of illness, but what moral or social significance contemporary culture attaches to the homosexual's behavior.
>
> Psychiatry's preoccupation with the disease concept of homosexuality conceals the fact that the homosexuals are a group of medically stigmatized and socially persecuted individuals. The noises generated by their persecution and their anguished cries of protest are drowned out in the rhetoric of therapy. It is heartless hypocrisy to pretend that physicians, psychiatrists or "normal" laymen for that matter, really care about the welfare of the mentally ill in general, or the homosexual in particular. If they did, they would stop torturing him while claiming to help him. But this is just what reformers, whether theological or medical, refuse to do.

As George Weinberg suggested in *Society and the Healthy Homosexual,* there is a serious problem leading to considerable pathological consequences that should concern psychologists and psychiatrists; the problem is not homosexuality as such but homophobia. The disease of homophobia is an attitude held by the majority of homosexuals themselves. "It is not surprising that the homosexuals themselves often suffer from the conventional attitudes of revulsion and anger toward things homosexual. In their case, the problem is even more serious than elsewhere—the attitude is a condemnation of the self." Weinberg believes that the essential issue is not whether one is homosexual but how the person handles his or her homosexuality. Consequently, a major task for therapists should be to determine why some people regarded as deviants remain tormented while others are able to go on and live successful lives.

The majority of authors dealing with the transitory character of many homosexual relationships and the prevalence of promiscuity among homosexuals recognize and have established beyond serious doubt that the primary reason for this negative quality in many homosexual liaisons is the guilt and self-hatred that so many homosexuals tend to internalize as a result of the judgment passed on them by society. As Dennis Altman observed in *Homosexual Oppression and Liberation* (New York: Dutton, 1971),

> Like the black, the homosexual suffers from a self-fulfilling stereotype. Tell people long enough that they are inferior, and they will come to believe it. Most of us are "niggers" because we believe that we are in large part what society constantly brands us as; in response, we come to exhibit the characteristics that justify our stigma. There are a large number of neurotic, unhappy, compulsively promiscuous homosexuals whom one might well regard as "pathological." This pathology is, however, the result of social pressures and the way they have internalized these, not of homosexuality itself. If people are led to feel guilty about an essential part of their own identity, they will in all likelihood experience considerable psychological pressures.

Many of the antigay psychiatrists mentioned manifest a very unscientific zeal in their effort to "cure" homosexuals. Some clinicians advocate what, from a Christian point of view, is a morally reprehensible procedure. Bergler, for example, speaks of "mobilizing any latent feelings of guilt." What he is advocating is a deliberate effort to increase the guilt feelings and self-hatred of the patient. Bieber, who goes along with this type of practice, reports only twenty-seven percent of his patients were "cured," by which he meant having heterosexual relationships.

One wonders what happened to the seventy-three percent who left therapy unconverted but burdened with false guilt and shame concerning their incurable condition. To hold out false hope of a change in one's sexual orientation in the light of almost total failure to truly effect a cure is morally reprehensible, for nothing can be more destructive psychologically than to hold out a false hope to an already despairing person. Connected with the issue of false hope is the danger of false guilt and shame in the majority of cases in which analysis fails to change sexual orientation. The great stress some clinicians place on a willingness to change as a necessary factor for the success of therapy has led many into further depths of self-accusation and despair. When that therapy fails, as it usually does, patients can easily draw the false conclusion that the failure was due to a fault of their will, for which they are morally responsible.

Over the twenty-plus years that I have been involved in positive gay therapy, dozens of the victims of these quack psychiatrists have ended up on my doorstep. They usually tell a tale of endless analysis with the idea that they could change their sexual orientation if they could unravel the oedipal fault that underlay their homosexuality. They recall the constant effort to increase their guilt and shame about their homosexual desires. Many were sent into electrical shock therapy to try to recondition their sexual response. Many others remember being sent to a skilled prostitute as part of their "therapy." Many had so interiorized guilt, shame, and self-hatred that the moment they felt a homosexual attraction they came close to psychotic breakdown. These unfortunate people were so damaged by their treatment that they had little hope of achieving a normal and happy life in their gay identity.

I also became aware over the years of so-called ex-gay ministries with the same tactics and the same destructive results. These ministries added the guilt that came from reading into scripture that homosexuality was condemned by God and could lead the practitioner into eternal hellfire. Courage, for example, a ministry officially sponsored by the Catholic church because it was in complete conformity with the Catholic ideological position, proposed that homosexuals have the "courage" to hate themselves and repress their homosexual desires. I am aware that many so-called ex-gays have not changed their sexual orientation but have repressed it out of self-hatred and guilt, with enormous devastation to their psychic health.

I was astounded and disgusted that *America* magazine, the Jesuit publication, gave over a recent issue to an article by Socarides, perhaps one of the most virulent and paranoid gay haters in the United States today. I am well aware that, since my expulsion from the Jesuits in 1988, my name has never appeared in the pages of *America*. They have listed all the theologians silenced by the Vatican, but my name was not included among them. They have never reviewed my last two books. It is obvious that, as far as they are concerned, I am a nonbeing. I can understand their fear of me, but I found their giving over their magazine to an article promoting hatred of gays incomprehensible and egregious. It is the moral equivalent of printing some pages from *Mein Kampf* in the 1930s.

This controversy among psychiatrists on the nature of homosexuality and its status as normal or diseased came to a head in December 1974, just as I was preparing my first book on homosexuality for publication. By a unanimous vote, the trustees of the American Psychiatric Association ruled (December 15, 1974) that homosexuality shall no longer be listed as a "mental disorder" in its official nomenclature of mental disorders. The category of "homosexuality" was replaced by "sexual orientation disturbance," which was described as follows:

> This category is for individuals whose sexual interests are directed primarily toward people of the same sex and who are either disturbed by, in conflict with, or wish to change their sexual orientation. This diagnostic category is distinguished from homosexuality, which by itself does not necessarily constitute a psychiatric disorder. Homosexuality per se is one form of sexual behavior and, like other forms of sexual behavior which are not of themselves psychiatric disorders, is not listed in this nomenclature of mental disorder.

During my many years of work with thousands of gays and lesbians, I have never discovered one person who actually made a *healthy* change in their sexual orientation. I have met many who have repressed their homosexuality and are trying to live out a false identity as heterosexual. I have come to the conclusion that one cannot change one's sexual orientation any more than one could change brown eyes to blue.

By a vote of 106 to 4 in September of 1997, the American Association of Psychologists charged that any effort to hold up a goal of changing sexual orientation in the light of the absence of any scientific evidence that such a change is possible would constitute "unethical practice" on the part of a therapist.

12

Launching Gay Ministry

As a result of my studies, I offered for publication an extensive research article, "The Christian Male Homosexual," to the *Homiletic and Pastoral Review*, a conservative magazine published as a pastoral resource for clergy. Previously in April and May of 1969, I had published in that journal a two-part article, "Joseph Fletcher on Sexual Behavior." In those articles, I argued against a cynical relativism proposed by the moralist Joseph Fletcher. I made the claim that all sexual activity is morally justified by the context of human love in which it takes place. The conditions of possibility for true human love were then the moral norms governing sexual activity. When the editor, Father Aidan Carr, received my manuscript on homosexuality, he wrote me that he had already made the decision to resign his post as editor to enter a contemplative order. Therefore, he was willing to take the risk of publishing my articles, which were published in three successive issues in 1970.

While I was composing these articles, Charlie went through a painful series of layoffs because of the electronics industry's moves to foreign shores and a severe general economic downturn. After exhausting the possibilities of obtaining a job in Syracuse so that we could stay together, in January of 1971, he moved to New Jersey and found employment in his field of electrical engineering. Fortunately, I was soon offered a new position as professor of Christian ethics at Woodstock Seminary, which had relocated a few years before from Woodstock, Maryland, to Riverside Drive in New York City, across from Riverside Church and Union Theological Seminary. I finished out the semester at LeMoyne College and moved to New York City in April 1971. I had a room at the Jesuit residence on Ninety-eighth Street. Most evenings, after my work was finished, I traveled by bus over to Newark to spend the night with Charlie in his apartment in the Colonnades. The warm support of Charlie's love made possible the burst of energy I experienced in my new assignment at Woodstock.

What a joy it was to be a part of the faculty at Woodstock, who welcomed me and encouraged me to continue my research and publishing! My fellow faculty members included Avery Dulles; Walter Burghardt, the editor of *Theological Studies*; Robert Springer, also in ethics; and Christopher Mooney, president of Woodstock and an expert on the thought of Teilhard de Chardin.

My first year at Woodstock, I was invited to join a task force sponsored by Fordham University on "freedom of conscience." This topic was studied simultaneously from theological, philosophical, psychological, and historical perspectives. I was asked to do a study of freedom of conscience from a theological perspective by using the philosophy of freedom of Maurice Blondel. This study was published in 1971 as *Conscience: Its Freedom and Limitations* (New York: Fordham University Press, 1971) and set the intellectual background for my *Freedom, Glorious Freedom*, which was to be published twenty-four years later.

The faculty at Woodstock invited me to take part in a collaborative effort to deal with the moral and theological issues involved in the new scientific discoveries in reproductive technology, such as in vitro fertilization. In response, I wrote what I still think is one of my best articles on the moral and theological issues of human freedom and its limits. That article, "Freedom and the Future," was published in the September 1972 issue of *Theological Studies*.

The next few years were the happiest and most productive of my stay in the Jesuits. Soon after arriving in New York, I received a letter from a group in Los Angeles called Dignity. They explained that the group had been founded a few years before as a Catholic organization for gay and lesbian Catholics. They had read my articles in the *Homiletic and Pastoral Review* and had drawn up a "Statement of Purpose" for the constitution of the organization based on my articles:

> A. We believe that Gay Catholics are members of Christ's Mystical Body, numbered among the people of God. We have an inherent dignity because God created us, Christ died for us, and the Holy Spirit sanctified us in Baptism, making us his temple, and the channel through which the love of God might become visible. Because of this, it is our right, our privilege and our duty to live

the sacramental life of the Church, so that we might become more powerful instruments of God's love working among all people.

B. We believe that Gays can express their sexuality in a manner that is consonant with Christ's teaching. We believe that all sexuality should be exercised in an ethically responsible and unselfish way.

C. As members of Dignity we wish to promote the cause of the Gay community. To do this, we must accept our responsibility to the Church, to Society and to individual Gay Catholics.

1. To the Church: to work for the development of its sexual theology and for the acceptance of Gays as full and equal members of Christ.

2. To Society: to work for justice and social acceptance through education and legal reform.

3. To individual Gays: to reinforce their self-acceptance and their sense of dignity, and to aid them in becoming more active members of Church and Society.

D. Dignity is organized to unite all Gay Catholics, to develop leadership and to be an instrument through which the Gay Catholic may be heard by the Church and Society. There are four areas of concern:

1. Spiritual Development: We shall strive to achieve Christian maturity through all the means at our disposal, especially the Mass, the sacraments, personal prayer, and active love of the neighbor.

2. Education: We wish to inform ourselves in all matters of faith as well as in all that concerns the Gay community so that we may develop the maturity of outlook needed to live fulfilling lives in which sexuality and spirituality are integrated, and to prepare ourselves for service in the Gay community.

3. Social Involvement: As Catholics and as members of Society we shall become involved in those actions that bring the love of God to others and provide the basis for social reform.

a. Toward Individuals: We wish to live a life of service to others, hoping to render visible the love of Christ and contributing our share to build a community of love.

b. With Gay groups: We wish to work with other Gay groups for the cause of justice to the Gay community and for the promotion of a sense of solidarity.

c. With religious and secular groups: We wish to work with them that they may better understand Gays and recognize present injustices.

4. Social Events: Activities of a social and recreational nature will be provided to promote an atmosphere where friendships can develop and mature, and where the Gay's sense of acceptance and dignity may be strengthened.

I was delighted with the way this group of extraordinary gay men in Los Angeles had translated my theoretical articles into a pragmatic program for action. I accepted their offer of honorary membership in their chapter and gave them permission to pass out copies of my articles to all the members.

Shortly after, I received a letter from a newly formed International Committee, which had been created to help form new chapters of Dignity all over North America. The letter was signed Gilgamesh. The letter writer's pseudonym was the name of the man in Babylonian creation mythology who fell in love with the wild man, Enkidou, the first recorded human love affair. Gilgamesh asked if I would be willing to help found a New York City chapter of Dignity. I investigated if there was a ministry in the diocese for gays and lesbians and found to my amazement there was none, despite the fact that New York City was the great mecca and refuge for gays and lesbians from all over the country and even the world. One bishop told me that the local parish was capable of meeting the spiritual needs of gays and that there was no need for a Catholic organization such as Dignity. Several years after Dignity was under way, the diocese tried to counter its influence by founding Courage and calling Father John Harvey in once a week from Virginia to run a meeting. It is my understanding that the average attendance at meetings of Courage was about twelve people.

During the summer of 1972, a group of us, priests and laymen, made our plans to begin Dignity New York. Both Joseph Killian (Gilgamesh) and Pat Allen flew in from Los Angeles to help us by sharing their experience in forming the first chapter in Los Angeles. Our first meeting was held in October 1972 at the church house of Trinity Episcopal Church. Our only publicity was a brief notice in *Village Voice* that an organization for gay and lesbian Catholics was in the process of formation, and we invited anyone who was interested to attend. With great apprehension, we anxiously awaited the response and had no idea how many would come. What an overwhelming sight it was when almost a hundred people showed up for that initial meeting! Obviously, what our group was proposing responded to a strongly felt need for so many gay and lesbian people. I told them at that first meeting, "Dignity is not something we can give ourselves, but it is something we can give each other!"

Dignity New York was off and running. Since that nervous beginning, it has met once a week every week for the last twenty-five years with average attendance of about two hundred. At least nine other chapters have grown out of Dignity New York, among them Dignity Big Apple, Brooklyn, Nassau County, Queens, Mid-Hudson, New Jersey Metropolitan, Jersey Shore, and Morristown. I served as provisional president of the chapter until we were able to organize an election.

The next couple of years were almost totally absorbed by organizing the chapter and its board and finding the direction for Dignity. As a matter of fact, I put in so much time and effort over many months at getting Dignity New York and subsequent chapters in many different locations going that it strained my relationship with Charlie almost to the breaking point. But, thank God, our love prevailed, and we were able to resolve the difficulties. Because so many gay Catholics were starving for this type of group support, Dignity chapters began springing up all over the United States. Of course, as Dignity became better known and its membership larger, I got into more and more hot water with the hierarchy, and Charlie and I had to be even more closeted.

The Woodstock Jesuit Community at Ninety-eighth Street and Broadway was totally cooperative with me in this ministry to lesbians and gays. The community gave Dignity its permission to use the chapel off the lobby for our liturgies and talks. The community also lent us their common rooms on the eighth floor for our social hour and provided free refreshments for all who came. This arrangement lasted for the first two years, a courageous act on the part of that community. It provided a safe home for Dignity until it was mature enough to go out and face the local churches' rejection in its search for a home of its own. St. John's Episcopal Church in Greenwich Village provided the first non-Catholic regular meeting place.

13

The Church and the Homosexual

Besides all the wonderful research projects I was part of at Woodstock Seminary during 1971, the theological faculty there urged me to expand my series of articles in the *Homiletic and Pastoral Review* into a full-fledged book. With that encouragement, I began the process that eventually resulted in the publication of *The Church and the Homosexual*, a process that lasted until 1976.

Once again I began further research on homosexuality. A friend at Union Theological Seminary provided me with a manuscript on the New Testament and homosexuality that argued that nowhere in the New Testament was there a clear condemnation of homosexuality. My friend told me that the author wanted to remain anonymous. I was able to incorporate much of this helpful document's argument into the manuscript of my book. (After the publication of the book I discovered that this manuscript was the work of John Boswell and was eventually published in his book *Christianity, Social Tolerance and Homosexuality* [Chicago: University of Chicago Press, 1980].)

When my manuscript was ready for publication, I searched for a publisher. The first seven I approached rejected the book. In fact, the editor of the Paulist Press called me in to upbraid me for challenging church teaching in this matter. I began to despair of ever finding a publisher.

Right at that time, I was invited to be the keynote speaker of the first national convention of Dignity, to be held in Hollywood, California, on Labor Day weekend in 1973. In my speech, I summarized all the evidence in favor of a moral reevaluation of homosexual relations. In its October 5, 1973, issue, the *National Catholic Reporter* (*NCR*) published the complete text of my speech and commented in its editorial that, because of a growing body of evidence, it was time for the church to reexamine its attitude toward the ho-

My father Charles's and Aunt Katie's wedding day, 1925. Back row (left to right): Tom; maid of honor; best man; my father Charles; and Katie. Front row (left to right): Francis, me, and Marion.

John McNeill,
high school graduation, 1942.

Home on leave, in Buffalo with my father, 1945.

Family portrait on the day I entered the Jesuit order (novitiate), August 1948. Back row (left to right): Me, Charles, Tom, Francis. Front row (left to right): Katie, Sister Sheila (Marion), my father Charles.

Group photograph taken on day of ordination at Fordham University, June 1959. Back row (left to right): Leon McNamara; John Sharkey and wife; Samuel Menashe; John Thornton; Hugh McFarland; John Kelley; Vivian (Tom's wife); Mary Jane (Francis's wife); Tom O'Connor, S.J.; Tom Fleming, S.J. Front row (left to right): Katie O'Gara, Mrs. Tom Sharkey, Sister Ernestine, Sister Sheila, me, Charles, Tom, Francis, Aunt Gertrude Soules.

Preparing to celebrate first mass at Fordham, 1959.

Celebrating mass (jeep is altar) for the American army in Germany, 1962.

John McNeill interviewed by Russell Barber on his NBC program, *First Estate*, 1976.

Lecture on "The Church and the Homosexual" at George Washington University, Washington, D.C., 1977.

Gay Rights Parade, New York City, 1982. Left to right: Fr. Dan McCarthy; Fr. Bernard Lynch; John J. McNeill, S.J.; Robert Carter, S.J.

With Phil Donohue after *The Donohue Show*, November 1986, on the occasion of breaking my silence.

Near my office at 98th Street and Riverside Drive, New York City, 1990.

At our home outside Deposit, New York, autumn 1992.

With my lover, Charles Chiarelli, in New York City, 1994.

My seventieth birthday party, 1995, at The Inn at Starlight Lake, Pennsylvania. Back row (left to right): Larry Kornfeld, Fred Dececchi, Ed Maybeck, Jim Wilbur, Timothy Mc-Neill, Judy McMahon, John McMahon. Front row (left to right): Linda Dececchi, Rose Dececchi (Charlie's sister), Charlie Chiarelli, me, Margaret Kornfeld, Susan Maybeck.

mosexual. What was needed, according to the editor, was "that the Church, individually and corporately, publicly and privately, should sit down with homosexuals and talk in an atmosphere characterized by enlightenment and compassion, not ignorance and invective."

The response to the *NCR* article was staggering. Literally hundreds of letters poured into my office, mostly requests for advice and inquiries about the forthcoming book from priests and religious who were attempting to counsel homosexuals. Finally, in January of 1974, I received a letter from Jim Andrews, of Sheed and Ward, offering to publish my manuscript. Almost simultaneously with that offer of publication, I received a notice from my Jesuit provincial that Father General Pedro Arrupé had written from Rome that I was not to publish anything in the popular press or to address homosexual groups. Officials told me later that, with the appearance of the article in *NCR*, pressure was brought to bear on Father General by various Roman congregations to take action against me in this matter.

I was particularly upset by this prohibition, first, because the implication of the letter that the moral debate could be carried on outside the notice of the public media and exclusively on an academic level was, in my judgment, totally impractical. Second, I was convinced that only through open discussion, with the Catholic homosexual community participating as an equal partner, could any real advance be made in the church's moral understanding of homosexuality and consequent pastoral services.

In the meantime, while participating in an all-day seminar on Christian sexuality sponsored by the Newark Diocese of the Episcopal Church, I was asked a question concerning homosexual marriage. I was reported in *The Living Church* magazine as approving "the liturgical solemnification of homosexual marriages." When this report reached Rome, pressure was again brought to bear on Father General. A second letter arrived in which I was forbidden to speak, publish, or teach anything on the question of homosexuality until a commission of theologians examined my writings. Jim Andrews agreed to keep his offer to publish my manuscript open until it was read and approved by the commission.

The commission was set up and received reports from my fellow Jesuit theologians Avery Dulles, Richard McCormick, and Robert Springer. An outstanding biblical scholar who has asked to remain anonymous and Charles

Curran of Catholic University also submitted reports. Although they did not necessarily agree with my arguments and conclusions yet, a majority of the commission reported that they found the manuscript a serious and scholarly work worthy of publication. Several felt strongly that there should be public debate on all the issues involved and that my manuscript would be an important contribution to that debate. One advisor even urged that as a matter of principle I should publish the book without submitting it to any form of prior censorship.

The commission's report was forwarded to Father Arrupé in Rome. He responded in April 1974 that he was grateful for the report of the commission but felt that a further step was needed. I was told by friends in Rome that Arrupé had hoped the whole affair could have been brought to an end by a negative report by the commission. Because circumstances had focused personal responsibility on the General to stress the need for me to be sensitive to the traditional norm of morality in my treatment of homosexual conduct, he requested that I forward a copy of the manuscript to Rome so that he could review it personally.

After waiting five months for an answer from Rome, I found out that the manuscript had never reached Father General's desk—it was deliberately lost in an overprotective secretary's desk drawer. I wrote to Father Vincent O'Keefe, an assistant to the General, who had been one of my favorite teachers at Woodstock. He hunted down the lost manuscript and saw to it that it arrived on the General's desk.

A coincidence happened just as my manuscript arrived on Father General's desk that I cannot help but view as providential. Several years earlier, while I was still at LeMoyne College, a new faculty member arrived, Jacqueline Ziegler, an artist and world-famous sculptor. She had spent the last few years in Africa with the Peace Corps, of which her husband had been director. I befriended Jacqueline and helped her move into her new position as director of fine arts. Jacqueline had been attracted to the Catholic faith since childhood, so she made the decision to convert from Judaism to Catholicism and asked me if I would instruct her in the Catholic faith and baptize her. She was baptized on the feast of St. Ignatius of Loyola in 1972. She sculpted a large bust of me as a gift, which adorns my living room to this day.

At the time my book arrived on Father General Arrupé's desk, Jacqueline arrived in Rome with a commission to sculpt a bust of Father Arrupé. Jacqueline enthusiastically told the General about the wonderful Jesuit priest who had befriended her, instructed her in the faith, and baptized her on the feast of St. Ignatius of Loyola, and his name was John McNeill. Father Arrupé, who probably knew little about me personally, could not help taking my book more seriously because of this glowing report about me.

Father Arrupé, I understand, submitted the manuscript of my book for critical review by a number of moral theologians in Rome. Once again, they gave very favorable reports and recommended that he allow me to publish the book. In October 1975, Father General turned over authority to give an *imprimi potest* (permission to publish) to the provincial of the New York Province of the Society of Jesus. He stated that he would not object to publication, granted that certain suggestions and guidelines made by the Roman censors be accepted and followed. Among the guidelines suggested was that another biblical scholar, whom he specified by name—the New Testament scholar Joseph A. Fitzmyer—should be consulted. When I called Father Fitzmyer and asked him to read my manuscript, he seemed angry at the request and let me know in no uncertain terms that he wanted nothing to do with it. When I informed him that he had been recommended by name by Father General, he responded, "Have him give me an order under holy obedience!" Instead, I sent the manuscript to William Thompson, S.J., of the Jesuit School of Theology in Chicago, who strongly supported the interpretation I had given to the New Testament passages and made the following observations:

> I find your treatment of the biblical data judicious and responsible. . . . You obviously have a sense of how an argument from Scripture about a current issue is to be developed. . . . Concerning methodological issues I could not agree more with your assessment of the impact of recent biblical studies in the Church on both dogmatic positions and moral/pastoral questions. . . . Consensus among theologians is not a matter of counting heads. It is a question of those who have understood and made operative in their theology the developments in biblical studies and those who have not.

Father General also requested, among other things, that I make clear where my manuscript differs from the traditional teaching of the church and that I omit the chapter on gay marriages. Having made all the changes demanded by Father Arrupé, we were ready to go into publication when yet another delay occurred.

The appearance of the document from the Sacred Congregation for the Doctrine of the Faith, "Declarations on Certain Questions concerning Sexual Ethics," in January 1976 called into question once again the granting of permission to publish. I was asked by my superiors to study the declaration and integrate what it had to say into my book.

I informed my superiors how I would respond to the declaration in my book and was delighted to receive a letter from my provincial, Father Eamon G. Taylor, S.J., on January 28, 1976, saying, "In my opinion the adjustments you have made to your manuscript in accordance with the agreement reached in our conversation of November 10th are responsive to the recommendations of Father General's letter of September 1975 and . . . as a result, I am happy to be able to grant the *imprimi potest*, as of this date."

14

Imprimi Potest

When I announced at the Dignity New York liturgy that I had received from my superiors in the Society of Jesus an official *imprimi potest*, the approval for the publication of *The Church and the Homosexual*, the joy we experienced that Sunday in 1976 was overwhelming.

In that book, I sought to refute three traditional stances taken by the Christian community regarding gay and lesbian relationships. I opposed, first of all, the view that God intends all humans to be heterosexual and that homosexuality therefore represents a deviation from God's divine plan—a deviation usually explained in terms of sin or, more recently, in terms of sickness. According to this view, those who find that they are lesbian or gay must change their orientation through prayer or counseling or, failing that, live totally celibate and sexually loveless lives. Sexual fulfillment thus becomes the exclusive right of heterosexuals. This was the position held in the Vatican letter "On the Pastoral Care of Homosexual Persons," issued in October 1986 to all the bishops of the world. That letter was deemed necessary to counter "deceitful propaganda" coming from the gay Christian groups that were challenging the church's tradition and its interpretation of scripture.

I suggested, instead, that God created human beings with a great variety of both gender identities and sexual-object choices. Consequently, the attempt to force humans into narrow heterosexist categories of masculinity or femininity can destroy the great richness and variety of God's creation. In all cultures and in every period of history, a certain percentage of men and women develop as gays and lesbians. These individuals should be considered as part of God's creative plan. Their sexual orientation has no necessary connection with sin, sickness, or failure; rather, it is a gift from God to be accepted and lived out in gratitude. God does not despise anything that God has created. Human beings do not choose their sexual orientation; they discover it as something given. To pray for a change in one's sexual orientation is about as meaningful as to pray for a change in the color of one's eyes. Furthermore, there is no healthy way to reverse or change sexual orientation once it is established.

Many Christian churches have limited their ministry to helping gay and lesbian people live out celibate lives. According to Christian tradition, celibacy is a special gift from God given to a certain few for the sake of God's kingdom. The occasional homosexual who receives this gift is indeed blessed because he or she can live in conformity with church teaching. Roman Catholic clergy choose a celibate way of life voluntarily, but lay people who are homosexual are given no choice; they are told that they must be celibate their entire lives under a threat of eternal condemnation.

There is no reason to believe that God grants this gift to everyone who happens to be lesbian or gay. On the contrary, empirical studies have shown that the vast majority of gay people who have attempted to live a celibate life end up acting out their sexual needs in promiscuous and frequently self-destructive ways. Every human being has a God-given right to sexual love and intimacy. Anyone who would deny that right to any individual must prove beyond all doubt the grounds for this denial. The only healthy and holy Christian response to a lesbian or gay orientation is to learn to accept it and live it out in a way that is consonant with Christian values.

The second thesis of *The Church and the Homosexual* was that homosexuals, rather than being a menace to the values of society and the family, have, as part of God's creative plan, special gifts and qualities and a very positive contribution to make to the development of society. Every family is blessed that has a gay son or lesbian daughter. In fact, they are the ones who usually take care of the parents in their old age. Indeed, if lesbians and gay men were to disappear, the further development of human society toward greater humaneness would be seriously endangered. Consequently, I conclude there is a special providence in the emergence of visible gay and lesbian communities within the church at this point in history.

The third thesis of this book was perhaps the most controversial. The church's traditional position had been that because every homosexual act is sinful and contrary to God's plan, the love that exists between gay and lesbian people is sinful and alienates the lovers from God. I argued that the love that exists between two gay men or lesbians, assuming that it is a constructive human love, is not sinful, nor does it alienate the lovers from God's plan. On the contrary, it can be a holy love, mediating God's presence in the human community as effectively as heterosexual love.

I naively assumed that by granting me an *imprimi potest*, the church, in the liberating spirit that followed Vatican II, was ready and willing to reexamine its teaching on homosexuality and that approving my book for publication was the first step in that process. The theologians who had reviewed my manuscript believed, as I did, that the new evidence coming from the fields of scriptural studies, history, psychology, sociology, and moral theology seriously challenged every premise on which the traditional teaching was based. They anticipated, as I did, that the book would begin a public debate on church teaching that eventually would lead to the church's revision of its understanding of homosexuality.

From the beginning, I envisioned the personal witness of lesbian and gay Catholics and other Christians to be an essential contribution to that debate. The church had to listen to what the Spirit was saying to them through the experiences of gay people. They would testify about what happened to them when they strove to live both as gays and according to church teachings. My own work in the gay community both as priest and psychotherapist and as one of the founders of Dignity New York made me keenly aware of the enormous amount of pain, psychological trauma, and potential emotional breakdown there. Because this unnecessary suffering was caused by the interiorization of self-hatred based in the church's teaching, I felt a certain urgency in the need for public debate. What was bad psychology had to be bad theology, and vice versa. Our early joy was short-lived, however.

15

The Media Response

My book immediately became a media event. Right after a press release conference held at the Harvard Club in New York City in September 1976, I appeared on the *Today Show* as its featured interview. It was Tom Brokaw's first day as host, and he was obviously uncomfortable with the subject. It was on the *Today Show* that I first came out of the closet and publicly acknowledged my own homosexuality. There were front-page stories in the *New York Times* and practically every other newspaper in the country and major stories in the "Religion" sections of *Time* and *Newsweek*. I appeared three times each on the *Phil Donahue Show* and *Larry King Live*. I toured more than twenty cities in the next year to do interviews for the press, radio talk shows, and local TV news and talk shows.

Of all the memorable events during that tour, two in particular stand out in my memory. The first occurred in Atlanta. Howard Wells, who had been my student at Union Theological Seminary during my time on the Woodstock faculty, and who had founded the New York City Metropolitan Community Church (MCC), a church for gays and lesbians, had become pastor of MCC in Atlanta. He had invited me down to Atlanta to give a three-day workshop on the theology of homosexuality. At the time, MCC Atlanta was located downtown in an old movie house. I was delighted, when Charlie and I arrived, to see my name and the topic on the marquee of the theater. While I was giving the series of talks, I noticed two muscular lesbians who were sitting against the wall at both sides of the stage. After the talks, Howard told me he hadn't wanted to worry me but there had been threats to disrupt the talks. The two women had ax handles on the wall behind them and were prepared to use them in case anyone stormed the stage. There was also a bulletproof-glass shield above the podium that could be dropped in front of me if anyone had threatened me with a gun. I probably was never more secure than I was there. Factually, nobody disrupted our three-day seminar, which was attended by several hundred people. Howard died a few years later.

The other incident occurred as a result of my visit to San Francisco. Dignity SF gave me a very warm reception. One of the many activities they organized was a long interview with me published in the *San Francisco Chronicle*. About two years later, I received a letter from a monk at a monastery in the city of Zamboanga on the island of Mindanao. He told me that he had come across the interview by accident as he unpacked books sent to the monastery library from the United States. The books were wrapped in newspapers, including the *Chronicle*. A gay man himself, he was delighted to learn there was a gay positive ministry being established for gays and lesbians. He had a vow of stability, which is a vow to remain within the walls of the monastery until death, but he intended to dedicate the rest of his life there in prayer for the success of this ministry.

The first sign that I was in trouble with the church occurred when I was in Cincinnati in 1976. I had been invited there by the theology department of Xavier University, a Jesuit school, to give a talk on the theology of homosexuality. It was the first time I encountered a large group of right-wing protesters; they surrounded the hall carrying placards denouncing the sin of sodomy. They were reciting the rosary, so at the beginning of my talk I had my audience recite a decade of the rosary with them to make the point that Mary was not necessarily on the other side.

I've always found it intriguing that gays are accused of committing the sin of sodomy when it is perfectly clear in scripture that the sin of sodomy was understood as inhospitality to strangers and mistreatment of the poor. In Ezekiel 16:49–50, we read, "This was the guilt of your sister Sodom: she and her daughters had pride, excess of food, and prosperous ease, but did not aid the poor and needy. They were haughty, and did abominable things before me; therefore I removed them when I saw it."

Even Jesus identified the sin of Sodom with inhospitality to the stranger:

But whenever you enter a town and they do not welcome you, go out into its streets and say, "Even the dust of your town that clings to our feet, we wipe off in protest against you. Yet know this: the kingdom of God has come near." I tell you, on that day it will be more tolerable for Sodom than for that town.

(Luke 10:10–12)

The homophobic interpretation of the sin of Sodom did not occur until the writings of the historians Philo and Josephus, near the end of the first century after Christ. They read back into the story of Sodom the homosexual practices they personally found so odious in the Greek city of Alexandria.

I have recently pointed out that what corresponds exactly to Ezekiel's understanding of the sin of Sodom and her daughters is the Republican "Contract with America."

At that time, Archbishop Joseph Bernadin (now the deceased Cardinal Bernadin of Chicago) was head of the diocese of Cincinnati. During the year of my visit to Cincinnati, Bernadin was elected president of the Conference of Catholic Bishops in the United States. I'd had one previous run-in with Archbishop Bernadin. In 1974, I was invited by the Marionist order in Dayton, Ohio, to give a conference on pastoral care of homosexuals for the priests of that order. The conference was held at Bergamo East, a retreat center near Dayton. The day before the retreat was to begin, the director of Bergamo East received a very angry call from Bernadin, who wanted to know why he had not been consulted before I was invited and asked if any media would be involved. The director told me that this incident was the first and only time the archbishop had interfered in the running of the retreat center.

While I was in Cincinnati for the conference at Xavier, the local chapter of Dignity held a banquet in my honor and gave me an award that read "For your courage, dedication and service to the gay community." They invited the archbishop, who responded that he had not read my book but, if the report in the September 20, 1976, *Time* magazine was accurate, he could not "in conscience" attend the banquet in my honor.

As I was leaving town, reporters from the local press read to me a press release sent to all media by Archbishop Bernadin in protest of my presence in Cincinnati:

> This weekend, Father John McNeill, S.J., will be in the city to speak about his new book, *The Church and the Homosexual*. Because his visit has already been given public notice and because his lecture will also be given publicity, I wish to restate the Church's position concerning homosexuality so that there will be no confusion in the minds of the people. . . . No one can take it upon himself to alter this clear teaching. While it is legitimate for theologians to explore this

moral question like any other, it is a disservice to challenge this teaching publicly in such a way as to give the impression that some radical change has taken place or is about to take place.

I responded to the reporters that I never once had suggested that the church had changed or was about to change its teaching on homosexuality. Rather, my public position was that the church *ought* to change its position, which was destructive to the health and happiness of hundreds of thousands of people. I left Cincinnati with a foreboding that I had not heard the last of this.

The importance of my book began to be recognized, and several foreign translations were published. The first was the Italian translation: *La Chiesa e l'omosessualità* published by Mondadori in 1976. It was the appearance of this translation that convinced the Curia in Rome that they had to make some move against me. The second was a translation into Danish: *Kirken og den Homosexuelle* published by the Niels Steensens Forlag in Copenhagen in 1978. The Danish publishers told me that every year the Catholic committee chose two books out of all the Catholic books of the past year to make available to the Danish-speaking populace. My book had been their first choice of all the books published in 1976. The third translation was Spanish: *La Iglesia ante La Homosexualidad*, volume 9 in the series Relaciones humanas y sexologia published by Grijalbo in 1979. The fourth was a French translation: *L'Église et L'Homosexuel: Un Plaidoyer* ("The Church and the Homosexual: A Defense"). The publishers, Labor et Fides, a Protestant publishing house in Geneva, felt so uncomfortable with the book that they included a critical review by Michel Demaison from a psychological perspective and Eric Fuchs from a theological perspective. Dorman and Todd in London published a special edition for the British Commonwealth.

In 1978, Simon and Schuster published a paperback edition, which sold out almost immediately. Unfortunately, Jim Andrews, who was my primary ally at Sheed, Andrews and McMeel, as the publisher was then known, died suddenly of a heart attack. Andrew had made a contract with me for a second book, but as soon as he died that contract was returned to me. Sheed, Andrews and McMeel discontinued printing my book, and there was no second printing of the Pocket Book edition, despite its success. I had a strong impression that someone was trying successfully to see that my book was taken out of circulation. My publishers continued, however, to hold on to the publishing rights. I had to wait until 1985 to free myself from the contract with Sheed, Andrews and McMeel and regain control of my book. I was able to get it back into circulation temporarily under Next Year Publications insignia. The book finally came back into print when Beacon Press republished it, together with my second book, *Taking a Chance on God*, in 1988. The book is now in its fifth edition at Beacon and still selling well twenty years after its initial appearance.

Another event shortly after the publication of *The Church and the Homosexual* has given a direction to my ministry to lesbians and gays for the past twenty years. Reverend Robert Raines, the director of the ecumenical retreat center at Kirkridge in the Poconos, read my book and decided to open his center to gays and lesbians. Kirkridge had been a support center for peace activists for many years. Bob contacted me and asked if I would be willing to conduct a retreat for lesbian and gay Christians in June of 1976. We have been conducting the annual retreats there ever since. Every year, close to a hundred people have gathered on the mountaintop to pray and share. For the past many years, Virginia Mollenkott, a lesbian spiritual leader, has joined me as coleader for the event. Other famous people in the field of gay spirituality who have joined us over the years as coleaders include Malcolm Boyd, Carter Heyward, Delores Williams, Chris Glaser, Beverly Harrison, Bill Smith, William Countryman, Scott Alexander, and many others.

The primary event in our Kirkridge retreat has been what we call the fishbowl. Ten people selected by the small groups sit in an inner circle and share their journey toward accepting their gayness and integrating it into a relationship of love with God. Of the hundreds of stories that have emerged from these fishbowls, I have observed a clear pattern of how God's love rescues gay and lesbian people from self-hatred and allows them to grow into a deep and joyously intimate relationship with God. About eleven years ago, I began a retreat for gay men also, called "Intimacy with God for Gay Men." This retreat, which takes place the first weekend in January after New Year's Day, attracts about a hundred participants annually. At present, I give about ten retreats a year all over the country.

16

Trouble! Trouble! Trouble!

In 1977, more than a year after the publication of my book, I was notified by my Jesuit provincial that the Vatican Congregation for the Doctrine of the Faith (CDF) had sent a letter to Jesuit Superior General Pedro Arrupé regarding my book. The congregation ordered that the *imprimi potest* be removed from future editions of the book. In addition, I was not to give lectures on homosexuality and sexual ethics or address the issue of homosexuality in the public media. When I called Jim Andrews and told him about this order from the Vatican, he refused to remove the *imprimi potest*. He insisted that Rome had to give him a good reason to do so, such as the book contained plagiarism or the scholarship was false. I requested a written account for this action. The request was refused. The provincial told me he had been forbidden by Rome to give me anything in writing. As a result, there was an outcry among church lawyers that I had been denied my right in canon law to receive a written account. But in its stead, in the summer of 1978, the CDF published in *Origens*, a periodical devoted to official church documents, a letter concerning my book. The letter, from Cardinal Ratzinger, the prefect of CDF, was addressed to Father Pedro Arrupé, the General, and explained the reasons why the congregation made the decision to silence me and remove the *imprimi potest*.

The letter began with a downright falsehood: "In his own words the author presents an 'advocacy theology.'" In my own words, in the preface to *The Church and the Homosexual*, I described how my critics had accused me of advocacy theology, but I denied that that was the case. I understood "advocacy theology" to be a biased and one-sided presentation of arguments, and I remarked in the preface that practically everything ever written on homosexuality, especially every statement from the Vatican, had been unquestionably advocacy theology. I stated, "For my part, I did my best to present fairly all the evidence for and against each thesis I dealt with. I never deliberately omitted or distorted any evidence even though it was contrary to my convictions."

The congregation's argument for removing the *imprimi potest* implied that I deliberately deceived my provincial, Eamon Taylor, and used Machiavellian means to get him to grant me the *imprimi potest*. Yet my manuscript was under censorship for more than five years. All the censors in both the United States and Rome agreed that there should be a public debate on the issues I raised.

While it is true that Father Taylor mentioned as one of his reasons for granting the *imprimi potest* that the book should be evaluated by my peers, there never was an understanding that I should somehow limit its distribution to the few dozen moral theologians in America. If that were the only intent for publication, I would have submitted an article to a professional journal, as I did several years previously with my articles on "the Christian male homosexual" in *Homiletic and Pastoral Review*. It would have been absurd to publish a book with a major publishing house with the idea of limiting its readership. Both Father Taylor and I thought that my book, because of its nature as a scholarly work, would not appeal to a large reading audience. Consequently, both of us were surprised when it became a best-seller and was translated and published in Danish, French, Spanish, and Italian.

I had been clear from the beginning with both Father Taylor and my peers that I thought no serious advance in moral thought concerning homosexuality could occur without dialogue with those who are living out that orientation and experiencing what the Holy Spirit says to them through their experience. To this day, it seems to me that the essential difference between the Vatican and me has to do with their distrust in the ability of the Holy Spirit to guide human conscience from within. Consequently, when I was invited to appear on various talk shows, I welcomed the opportunity and was in no way in conflict with the agreements I made with my superiors.

I feel sure that Father Taylor, when he wrote in the letter granting the *imprimi potest* about my peers studying my work, believed that my book would receive severely critical and negative reviews from other moral theologians, but such did not prove to be the case. On the contrary, most reviews were very favorable and welcomed my book as a breath of fresh air. Father Taylor was so perplexed by this reaction that at one point, a year after publication of the book, he telephoned me and asked if I myself could somehow arrange to have some negative critical reviews published. I had the impression that request originated in the General's office in Rome.

The letter also accuses me of "the gravest sort of disregard for the mature study and loyal support for the authentic magisterium of the church" because my book was published only a few days after the publication of *Persona Humana*, a document dealing with sexual ethics in general and homosexuality in particular. The letter again failed to mention that on pages 11 to 16 in *The Church and the Homosexual*, I do discuss the document, which I refer to in the text as "The Declaration on Certain Questions concerning Sexual Ethics." But because the document was merely a restatement of the classical condemnation of homosexuality based on a distorted homophobic reading of scripture and the so-called natural law and there was no new argument or position that I had not already fully treated in the text of my book, there was no need to discuss it at greater length. I stated the argument of the document and asked my readers to judge whether I had adequately responded to it.

Finally, the congregation quoted the press release of Archbishop Bernadin on the occasion of my visit to Cincinnati in 1977, which I discussed earlier. It was obvious from this series of events that the congregation felt that they were losing the argument and, therefore, fell back on asserting their authority and trying to silence any debate.

At the time I received this order from the CDF to silence on the issue of homosexuality, I made the immediate decision to obey it in accordance with my special vow of obedience to the Vatican. At the same time, I decided to enter into a process of prayer and discernment to try to discover what God's Spirit wanted me to do. I had not, however, been denied the right to continue my direct ministry to gays.

When I was silenced, I was scheduled to give the keynote address at the 1977 National Dignity Convention in Chicago. I sent an open letter to the delegates explaining why I had chosen to obey the order and was therefore canceling my scheduled speech. In the letter, I said:

> I think it is important to note what is *not* being said in the directive. It does not in any way demand a retraction or a repudiation of my ideas or judgments in this book. After a great deal of prayer and consultation I personally have made

the decision to obey the directive. It was always my hope and my dream that through my scholarship and efforts, I could make some contribution to a reconciliation of the Church with the gay community and the gay community with the Church. At this time and under these circumstances I now judge that the best contribution I can make to that dream is by my silence. I hope by my silence to be of service both to the Church which I love and the gay community with which I have become so closely identified.

I hope also that my silence will be eloquent. I hope it will join the silence of those many theologians and philosophers of pre–Vatican II, Maurice Blondel, Teilhard de Chardin, John Courtney Murray, Henri de Lubac and many others whose obedience eventually led to their vindication. I would like my silence in some way to symbolize the defenseless silence through the centuries, and even today, of hundreds of thousands gay Catholics.

John J. McNeill
September 1977

Charlie and I did not, of course, attend that convention, but instead we went to Provincetown on Cape Cod to avoid any possible publicity or contact with the media. When Charlie proofread the statement I wrote to send to the Chicago convention, he said he hoped my vindication would occur sooner than it had for Galileo.

During those nine years of being silenced in the public media, several events changed my life. The first was the closing of Woodstock Seminary. The decision was made in Rome, due to a drop in vocations, to reduce the number of Jesuit seminaries in the United States from five to three. Woodstock was originally chosen to be among the survivors. The oldest Catholic seminary in the United States, it predated the formation of the republic. It had an extremely talented and respected faculty, and it was at the center of a new commitment to urban ministry. Weston Seminary in Massachusetts appealed the decision that it should be closed. A new process began, and the decision was reversed: Woodstock was to be closed, and Weston would remain open. To the best of my knowledge, this reversal of decision was based on the fact that Weston had a firm commitment from Harvard Divinity and other seminaries in Cambridge to form a consortium. Weston also had a centralized community, whereas Woodstock's students were spread over several residences in apartment houses on New York's upper west side. The rumor has gone around that Woodstock was closed because of its welcome to Dignity and the homosexual community, but I believe the decision to close Woodstock was made long before Dignity began to meet at Woodstock.

It was heartbreaking to close the door and turn off the lights after 150 years of tradition. I have always thought that the decision to close Woodstock was a serious error on the part of Rome. The Catholic church in the United States lost its primary center of theological scholarship and research, and the only intelligent and sophisticated voice of the church in the New York City area, with its concentration of media, was silenced.

I applied as professor of ethics to various Jesuit colleges and universities with no response. I discovered later that the Roman Congregation on Colleges and Universities had blacklisted me.

17

Healing Ministry

My work with Dignity had made me aware that I lacked the professional skills to do the kind of counseling that its members needed. With Charlie's encouragement, I requested permission from my provincial to return to school and complete a postgraduate program in psychotherapy at the Institutes of Religion and Health.

The Institutes had been founded by a psychiatrist, Smiley Blanton, and Norman Vincent Peale. It is located in the church building behind Marble Collegiate Church on Twenty-ninth Street in New York City. The Institutes came into existence to train clergy of all denominations in the skills of psychotherapy. It was the first of its kind. Because it was the policy at most psychotherapeutic training programs not to accept an openly gay student, I took the risk of applying as a gay man. I wanted the training they could give me to help me in my ministry to lesbians and gay men. The Institutes accepted me. Shortly after, the faculty formed a committee to draw up a policy on admission of lesbian or gay students, and I was invited to serve on that committee. What a relief it was to be in a community of adults where this issue could be dealt with in an open, aboveboard, and intelligent way!

I am still profoundly grateful for the opportunity the Institutes offered me. First of all, there I was, fifty years old and beginning a new career with a group of clergy and laypeople, most of them in their thirties, bright, competent, compassionate people who wanted to dedicate their lives to lifting the burden of suffering from people with psychic problems and free them for a full and happy life. While most people my age were looking forward to retirement, I was just beginning a new and exciting career. The faculty was excellent; the training in all fields of therapy—individual, couples, and group—was the best available. At times, I felt that I was in the equivalent of the Harvard of train-ing institutes.

The school wisely recognized that the primary path to a deep, personal knowledge of how therapy cured was to personally participate in as thorough a therapeutic experience as possible. For the first time, I underwent therapy treatment of my own; it was a requisite for training. I had the good luck of choosing as my therapist Arnold Rachman, a brilliant, insightful, and com-passionate man. For the next four years, we worked together twice a week on individual therapy and once a week in a group therapy session. I had no idea how badly wounded I had been in my childhood—by the death of my mother, by my father's emotional absence, and by the trauma of growing up as a self-hating gay man. With Arnold's skilled help, I was able to raise most of those issues to consciousness and free myself from their pathological grip on my life. Through my own therapeutic process, I learned firsthand the skills I would need to help other gay people.

As soon as I graduated from the three-year program, the Institutes hired me as a faculty member and then as director of its pastoral ministries program, a program designed to provide inner-city clergy of all denominations with coun-seling skills in their ministries. My experience in this program opened my eyes to the ethnic and cultural differences in dealing with psychological issues with various groups. A few years later, I was invited to join the faculty to teach the-ory of psychotherapy to the second-year students. This teaching post allowed me to combine my background in philosophy with an in-depth study of all post-Freudian development of psychoanalytic theory. I personally chose the Object Relations school—the school of Fairbairne, Winnicott, and Gun-trip—as the primary focus in my classes on theory. This school believes that the primary childhood wounding of the psyche resulted from the kind of re-lationship the child had with parenting figures. Therefore, the primary cura-tive element in therapy was linked to the nature of the relationship that developed between client and therapist. We were involved in reparenting our clients in an atmosphere of compassionate love, redoing the superego, bring-ing unconscious patterns into consciousness, and freeing the client to live a full life of love and relationship.

During this period of training, I persuaded my Jesuit superiors to allow me to rent an apartment on Ninety-eighth Street and Riverside Drive as my residence and office. I needed to change my official residence from the Jesuit Community at Ninety-eighth and Broadway, and it was only a few blocks away. I had to move because many of my clients were priests and religious. If they were to come to see me as a therapist at the Jesuit Community, they could not come and go undetected by the rest of the community. Because the nature of my practice with gays was well known, they therefore would have risked "coming out."

Charlie and I moved into the Ninety-eighth Street apartment in 1977. That was the first time in the twelve years of our relationship that we were able to live together. I quickly built an active private practice as therapist and spiritual director. I also developed a group therapy practice for gay men. I have spent the last twenty years of my life doing the combined works of teaching, giving retreats and workshops, and therapy. I am grateful to God for leading me out of the sterile confines of left-brain academia and into this new life-giving and life-serving work.

18

Support of My Jesuit Brothers and My Peers

During the nine years that I was silenced, I struggled daily through prayer and consultation to try to find God's will for me. My Jesuit Community at Ninety-eighth Street and Broadway was a great help to me in that process. Every few months, the CDF issued a new order restricting me further. To relay the new demands to me, the provincial phoned or wrote to me and ordered me to meet with him at his office on the Fordham campus in the Bronx. Every time I saw another letter from the provincial, I went into a deep depression, and, because there was usually a week between being summoned and taking the trip to Fordham, I faced a week laden with anxiety, sleepless nights, and diarrhea. Then I set out on my *via dolorosa*, taking the Number 1 train to Columbus Circle, the F train to Fordham Road, then finally the long walk to the provincial's residence on Fordham Road at the edge of Fordham University.

Each visit resulted in ever more narrowly tightened restrictions of my ministry to gays and lesbians. During one meeting, I was told that my conjunctive interpretation of the prohibition on me "not to speak on homosexuality *and* sexual ethics" was unacceptable. I had interpreted that order as giving me permission to speak on homosexuality if I did not speak concurrently on sexual ethics or, conversely, I was free to speak on sexual ethics if I did not mention homosexuality. On still another occasion, Father Dezza, who was appointed by Pope John Paul II as the papal inquisitor to replace Father Arrupé, wrote to tell me that I was forbidden to address the issue of homosexuality from any viewpoint, even including that of psychology or spirituality. Sometimes during our meeting, the provincial found it necessary to bring in my dossier to consult some disputed communication. I was amazed to see that the dossier was well over a foot thick.

I am grateful for the continued support I received during those painful years from my Jesuit Community at Ninety-eighth Street. Every time I received a new order from Rome, I would ask the community to join me in a prayerful discernment process. Especially helpful to me were my spiritual advisor, Robert Springer, and my Jesuit brother Daniel Berrigan. At one point, someone told me that, as a result of my ministry to gays, the Vatican might take punitive action against the Society of Jesus. Attacked by feelings of guilt and self-pity, I drew up a letter resigning from the Society of Jesus, thinking that I should protect it against the danger of my presence. When I read the letter to my community in a discernment meeting, they were upset and unanimously recommended that I not send the letter. Daniel Berrigan, in particular, strongly suggested that I leave the decision to expel me to Jesuit superiors and let them take responsibility for their decision to support me or to give in to the Vatican. On their advice, I tore up that letter and wrote instead that I intended to continue my ministry and expected my superiors in Rome to defend my right to do so.

During my enforced silence, an important and powerful voice was raised in my defense. I am profoundly grateful to Daniel Berrigan, S.J., for having the courage to speak out on my behalf during those years of silence and struggle with Rome. After one of our discernment sessions, Dan asked to see all the documents that had passed between me and Rome. After studying them, he published an article in *Commonweal*, December 9, 1977, "The Leveling of John McNeill." He later included it as a chapter of his book *Portraits of Those Whom I Love*, under the title "The Jesuit" (New York: Crossroads, 1984).

In the preface to his book, Dan explained his reasons for including me among his portraits:

> Some of us have learned a few things: that friendship in the nature of things human or divine tends to the particular. Those who leap the first barrier (Thou shalt not!), then make a further discovery: Certain canonical prohibitions, implicit or clearly spelt out, which excluded women, gays, others, from the common table, font or anointing, were as inhuman and spiritually destructive as the earlier "thou shalt not" aimed at the heart of our youth.
>
> It was at this second barrier that I met John McNeill. In the middle sixties, I had been tossed about boisterously in the grab bag of fortune for daring to surmise aloud that the Vietnam war was not exactly America's or Christianity's finest hour. Years later, along came John. He was employed, so to speak, in ap-

plying a lever against a lid of a can of dark and living surmises. And for this, it was decreed, he was to be tossed to oblivion likewise. Thus, two soldiers of misfortune met, the friendship goes on, trouble and redemption in uneasy passage.

Dan begins his chapter "The Jesuit" with a quote from Kierkegaard's *The Present Age:*

> While a passionate age storms ahead, setting up new things and tearing down old, raising and demolishing as it goes, a reflective and passionless age does exactly the contrary. It hinders and stifles all action. It levels. . . . Enthusiasm may indeed end in disaster, but leveling is *eo ipso* the destruction of the individual. No age, and therefore not the present age, can bring the skepticism of that process to a halt. For as soon as it tries, the law of the leveling process is again brought into play. Leveling can only be halted by the individual attaining the religious courage, which springs from his individual religious solitude.

Dan talks about the "heady romanticism" of the sixties, when we felt that everything was possible to us. The passionate age of the sixties was succeeded by the Great Leveler:

> The point of all this is to suggest a contrast. On the one hand, the levelers. On the other, the out of tune, out of joint, out of step character named by Kierkegaard "the religious individual." This one has no sense of right timing, cannot read traffic signs, has indeed no interest in reading them, is utterly and incurably irrelevant (to all but one thing), speaks up when everyone urges equivocal prudence, is silent in the midst of hot contention, has no authority beyond the useless currency of human concern. He (she) has only the simplest of projects to commend him: a project that arose from walking in the world and observing events there. It might be put like this: to save or aid one other person, or a few. The project, of course, makes little sense in an age leveled off to hot crowds and shifty crowd pleasers.

Dan speaks of me as the "sore thumb" that tells us of the condition of the body: the pain of one member is to the honor of all, a sign to be winced at.

> One Jesuit held up his pain (and ours) before the befuddled public gaze, a gaze that quickly, in official eye sockets, has darkened with horror. Consider the case. A Doctor of Philosophy in the time-honored mold, teacher, writer, counselor. To this point, no pain: all well and good. I met John McNeill years ago in Europe. He was undergoing the grueling obstacle race *honoris causa* at Louvain. Our paths crossed briefly, as I recall, in Paris. We got on well. He was amiable, alive in the mind; certainly we were both great innocents, with the dreadful,

uncharted future laying out there, and we bemused, thinking our lives would go straight as the arrow of God's (purported) will: safe, sound, bell, book, candle, cassock, rule, long black line, classroom, rec room, womb-to-tomb security.

It's all gone for good: in more senses than one. Now he is grizzled as Zero Mostel; he has the look we all wear, except for a few chic hangers-on, the look of bare survivors, of a wreck that went under like a stone. We're surprising to ourselves; we don't know how we made it ashore; couldn't tell if asked. John is unacceptable in his field—ethics—to any Catholic university in the land, Jesuit included. I'm somewhat less immediately notorious. But the security, the credit cards, the sound ID went down in the catastrophe referred to above. Now we live by our wits so to speak.

Dan mentions reading over the letters from Rome and compares them to "last week's omelet; cold but wholesome, with a cross cut into their flab to render them less indigestible." He speaks of them as urging repentance, submission, silence, withdrawal—"the conduct generally befitting repentant children snatched by adult hands from lapse or lunacy." He mentions the exception of Father General Arrupé's letters, "whose humanity breaks through." Dan continues:

Bizarre goings-on are transpiring, not isolated events, a crazy continuum, America, now. The Jesuit McNeill, on the threshold of distinction, an expert in ethics, a man well loved, held in respect—such a one begins speaking up on behalf of homosexuals. Not content with keeping closet matters where in decency they belong, and keeping such people where they belong, and urging on them contentment with their lunatic lot—no, he refuses that way, which is the time-honored way, the way the church has invariably gone, so that matters that belong in the light may stand in the light, and other unlovely, barely mentionable matters may dwell where fate (correction, God's will) assigns them: in the shadow. This Jesuit refuses to follow that way. He takes a few of these people by the hand and leads them into the very center of the circle—the circle, let us say of worship, of brother and sisterhood. He introduces them to other Christians: he blesses them, shrives them, communicates them, just like the others. Everything is seemly and normal and above board. In Christ, he says, there is neither hetero nor homo, but one Body, His own.

Now this activity approaches the dangerous, and some people wince, and mutters of disaffection are heard. John seems not to hear them. If he does hear them, he grants them no attention. He is, as I suggested, one of Kierkegaard's *enfants terribles,* a "religious individual," out of tune, out of step. He has held a hand in his own, has sensed human suffering, has witnessed injustices, psychic destruction, stigma, rejection. From this gesture he takes the measure of the world, the measure of church teaching, the measure of his own soul. And so he walks one step further. It is not that he is ignorant, that he does not know that he is on thin ice. Rather, he makes small account of such things; or at least (there is no point in creating a fiction here, a human without fear) he makes less account of personal danger than of the untended and unmerited suffering that his "prudence" would only worsen.

Dan then retells the history of my effort to publish *The Church and the Homosexual*:

> But what followed is probably one of the most extended eking-out of reluctant approbation in all the slow turning of the Roman mills. In those months and years, I saw a new side of McNeill: the strength of absolutely marmoreal patience. To this day, I am trying to absorb and understand it. He waited, he questioned, he was rebuffed, he waited, once more he was told to wait, he was counseled to be patient by millennial-minded authorities. His manuscript was scrutinized by enough experts to sanitize the Aegean stables. Their fine tooth comb declared him again and again tick-free, lice-free, dandruff-free; gnat or camel, they could find nothing to stick at. Through it all he was unfailing, exasperatingly courteous, a gentleman *ad unguem*. I watched and marveled and began to think the lapsarians wrong. Here was a Jesuit who escaped the lamentable common fate, when our garden became a spoiled playground. Where was his rancor, exasperation, his coil and recoil, the sweat and bruises we all bear into the public arena?

Dan proceeds to a radical criticism of the church as failing in its task of bringing the liberating message of God's love to gay people: "That which should confer faith and hope and charity, poisons us with bad faith, diminishing our hope to the vanishing point, comes toward us small and sour of mind." Once again Dan takes a critical distance from me in terms of my (supposed) lack of anger at the time Rome silenced me:

> But these reflections are meant to be an act of love. I am not sure I find McNeill's response to my crude taste. It is somewhat too mystical, it takes refuge, it is not angry. I hope he is not too resigned, just as I am sure he is not hateful. But apart from all that, I honor him. Today, when every conceivable question is politicized out of its reasonable skull, he places a sure, patient, obscure sense of soul above every crude feint or ploy. I suspect his sense of history is sound, and this not merely a tactic. I think he is unafraid of the cross.

What has always impressed me about Daniel and his peace ministry, be-yond his incredible courage and self-sacrifice, is his certainty. There is an es-sential difference between Dan's ministry and mine. There is a two-thousand-year tradition, beginning with Jesus himself, that places Dan's peace work on the side of the angels. Father General Arrupé flew from Rome to spend a day of prayer with Dan in his prison cell in Danbury, Connecticut. And Dan's pic-ture was on the front of a recent issue of *America* (April 27, 1996) to celebrate his seventy-fifth birthday, and he is still a member of the Jesuits. There never was a moral issue involved in Dan's ministry—prudential issues on tactics, yes, but immorality, no.

It's quite a different question when the ministry involves homosexuals and must deal with the two-thousand-year history of homophobia both in dis-torted translations of scripture and in tradition. One cardinal in Rome made the comment in reference to my first book, *The Church and the Homosexual:* "Who does he think he is? King John giving the Magna Carta to homosexu-als to be able to practice their vices?"

Another essential difference between us has to do with the fact that I am a gay man myself. We never discussed sexual orientation, but I strongly suspect that Dan is a heterosexual. I never heard that Dan needed years of psychother-apy, as I did, to heal the psychic wounds of growing up gay. Dan's problem was primarily outside him. My problem was a dimension of myself. We who grew up gay had a particular problem with anger. In our youth, in order to survive, we had to learn never to express our anger freely but to turn it in on ourselves. We learned to keep mother and father good, keep authorities good, keep the church good. We immediately understood what D. W. Winnicott meant when he wrote in *The Maturational Process and the Facilitating Environment: Studies in the Theory of Emotional Development* (New York: International Universities Press, 1965): "Every child knows in its heart that it would rather be a devil in a world ruled by a good God, than a saint in a world ruled by Satan."

Anger is psychic pain. We are necessarily angry as long as we are wounded. If we can heal the wounds, then we can let go of the anger in a healthy way. Through therapy I was able to begin to heal most of my psychic wounds, but it was primarily through my prayer life that I dealt with anger. If in my morn-ing session of centering prayer I had an intense experience of God's love for me, with that experience my wounds were healed and my anger flew out the window. Certainly, my intimate human love with Charlie for thirty-two years was also a source of great healing for me. There was one form of anger, how-ever, that has motivated my work all my life, the anger at injustice and un-necessary human suffering.

At the end of his article, Dan addressed the following message to me:

Dear Brother John McNeill,

We shall have to content ourselves with perhaps two simple acts, which I take it are nearly all we can do today. First of all we must continue to slip the chains and bonds from our hands (and feet and tongues and souls). This idea is too simple to need developing. We can go along with their silencing us; we can go along to their jails; but we must do these things with our passionate hearts, for our good reasons, for our people, knowing our cause is just and worthy and speaks for all. We must not go in their direction hangdog, like dogs to their own hanging. And second, we must offer strange gifts to authority. And the best gift that I can think of is our own rebirth, our liberation. Something embarrassing, something sublime; come along the freedom road!

Another statement of support that meant a great deal to me came from the Theology Council of the Jesuit School of Theology in Chicago, dated January 10, 1978:

1. We, the undersigned of the Theology Council of the Jesuit School of Theology in Chicago, after serious deliberation, respectfully request the Holy See to permit Father John J. McNeill, S.J., to resume his academic and pastoral ministry within the area of Sexual Ethics—a ministry denied him by the recent action of the Sacred Congregation for the Doctrine of the Faith.

2. In many pronouncements from the Ecumenical Council, the Synod of Bishops and the Holy Father, justice has been emphasized as an integral part, indeed a constitutive element of the preaching of the Gospel. To prepare to pro-claim the demands of justice to the world, the Church has acknowledged its own need "to undertake an examination of the modes of acting . . . in the Church . . . to the end that in the Church itself rights must be preserved." Fur-thermore, "in the Church as in other institutions and groups, purification is needed in internal practices and procedures . . . whose violations of human rights deserve censure." "No one should be deprived," according to the Synod of Bishops in 1971, "of his ordinary rights because he is associated with the Church in one way or another. . . ."

These rights include, first, the freedom of the children of God. The Pastoral Constitution, *Gaudium and Spes* (n. 62), of the Second Vatican Council mandates, "Let it be recognized that all the faithful, clerical and lay, possess a lawful freedom of inquiry and of thought and the freedom to express their minds humbly and courageously about those matters in which they enjoy competence." This freedom has been summarily denied to Father McNeill. These ordinary rights also include the right to a warning before censure and judicial procedure that "Should give the accused the right to know his accusers and also the right to a proper defense." Father McNeill has received none of these basic rights in the process that led to his silencing. Moreover, the Second Vatican Council asserts that "the truth cannot impose itself except by virtue of its own truth. . . ." The recent action of the CDF rather than establishing truth has made the truth inaccessible by denying Father McNeill the right to continue to expose his positions to the criticisms of other theologians in that process of rational discourse which is perhaps the richest heritage of the Roman Catholic Church. In its place the Congregation has tried to impose truth by coercive force, a process always condemned when it is attempted by civil government.

3. The Common Good, according to traditional moral theology, is the overriding goal of all authoritative enactments. Rather than supporting the common good, the action against Father McNeill impedes the common good. In the first place, both his colleagues and those who have received his care in and out of the Gay Community attest to the grace and truth of his pastoral ministry and his adherence to the Church's time honored norms for its pastors. The men and women of the Gay Community have been deprived of an able and trusted pastor. This is especially tragic in a time when the Catholic Church had already lost most of its credibility among a group of people who are especially in need of the preaching of the love of Jesus Christ and the power in the Holy Spirit for good, as they face a hostile world. Instead, they are left profoundly discouraged by the Congregation's action. Secondly, the common good has been damaged by the flagrant lack of due process and the coercive and summary suspension of ordinary human freedoms. In the United States of America, a country where due process and freedom of speech are the very cornerstone of political life, this action against Father McNeill causes the gravest political scandal and is easily construed as invalidating any right the Catholic Church might have to preach justice and reform in secular affairs.

4. Moreover, the silencing of Father McNeill poses a threat to all Roman Catholic academic ministry in the United States. The freedom required for responsible service to the truth (cf. the AAUP Statements on Academic Freedom and Tenure, and on Professional Ethics) has been denied to Father McNeill. This is all the more distressing since, in conformity with Roman Catholic practice, his work has been humbly and obediently submitted to qualified censors who found it not out of conformity with sound teaching. Furthermore his work

had been offered as an academically competent and bona fide attempt to contribute to the development of Roman Catholic teaching on sexuality. Persons outside the church are scandalized and moved to question the integrity of all Catholic research, writing and teaching. Persons within the Church are unnecessarily threatened and hindered in their academic ministry by this action against one who has proceeded humbly, obediently, prudently, responsibly, and in all good faith.

5. In conclusion, it should be noted that Father McNeill has accepted the action of the Sacred Congregation in all meekness and silently, imitating the action of many great and holy scholars and pastors inside and outside of the Society of Jesus. This in itself argues eloquently in his behalf and moves us to urge that he be given quick assurance of his freedom to resume his rightful ministry as scholar and pastor. This action will hearten every truly devout Catholic engaged in ministry, especially academic ministry, in the United States.

Voted in the Theology Council of the
Jesuit School of Theology in Chicago,
Meeting on January 10, 1978
(15 for, 0 against, 6 abstain)

News of this support from my Jesuit brothers in Chicago came as a complete surprise, and I was moved to tears. I had no expectations of receiving such strong support from within the society. Up until then, all I had experienced from fellow Jesuits concerning my gay ministry, with the exception of those in my community who supported me, was downright hostility and indifference at best.

At the time of my silencing, one of the attacks against me in Rome brought into question my competence as a psychotherapist, so the support I received from my colleagues at the Institutes of Religion and Health was very important to me. These were the people who were closest to me and knew my work well. For example, at my request, Robert E. Svenson, president of the Foundation for Religion and Health, my former teacher and supervisor, wrote the following letter to my provincial, Vincent Cooke.

August 1, 1983
Dear Father Cooke:

I am writing on behalf of John McNeill, who has requested that I inform you to the best of my knowledge concerning his work.

I have known Father McNeill since 1975, when he was first a student at the Blanton-Peale Graduate Institute. Father McNeill also taught in our Pastoral Studies Program upon his graduation from the Institutes.

John was and is one of the finest teachers that we had in our Pastoral Studies Program. The program is run for clergy and religious, and focuses on counseling in a parish setting. John continues to be one of our most popular teachers. He is articulate, is able to connect with the students, and is able to integrate theology and psychotherapeutic techniques in a way that few are able to do.

I have also supervised John over the past several years in his clinical work. In his work with clients, John is warm, caring and empathetic. He does solid clinical work and addresses people at their deepest spiritual level. Many clients who come to us as pastoral counselors come to see us because they are in enormous spiritual conflict. John, in his work with clients, helps them resolve these conflicts in order for them to become better participants in the work of the Church.

Personally speaking, I must say that John is one of the finest Christian men that I know. I know in my work many ministers, priests and rabbis and there are few that I know that can so articulate the faith in a tone that really reaches out to people as John can. I know that he has worked a lot with the gay community. John has not set himself up as judge of any other person. From my perspective, what he does is offer people an opportunity to work through their conflicts within the confines of the counseling center.

Sincerely yours:

The Rev. Robert E. Svenson, President

My professional peers at the Institutes elected me president of the Alumni/ae Association and in 1989 presented me with the Distinguished Alumnus Award, which read:

This special tribute acknowledges John McNeill as a priest, teacher, therapist, ethics and moral theologian, author, and as a leader for gay and lesbian liberation. His humanity breaks through the cultural norms to reach the outcast facilitating spiritual health and psychic healing. He has demonstrated uncommon courage and uncommon travail walking where few would go, sensing human suffering, injustice, psychic destruction, stigma, and rejection, and responded to those in need of acceptance and healing. John is a person of integrity who has not hesitated to embrace the difficult task of defending that which is morally right at the risk of losing that which is important to him personally.

We support your cause, we have been released from our bondage by knowing you, and we know in our hearts that your cause is just and worthy.

The Alumni/ae of the Institutes are professional psychotherapists, most of whom are themselves clergy of all denominations. Their support and approval in the end meant more to me than any a priori condemnation of my work coming from the Vatican.

Dan's article and the support of the Jesuit Theology Council and of my peers at the Institutes buoyed me up for the next many years of painful silence.

On November 13, 1993, the Eastern Region of The American Association of Pastoral Counselors granted me their distinguished contribution award: "To our colleague, mentor and voice from the wilderness. Our region has been enriched by your healing prescence and skillful practice of pastoral psychotherapy, by your wisdom imparted as supervisor, author, and teacher of pastoral psychotherapy and spiritual direction, by your prophetic message to us from gays and lesbians who have discovered their spiritual gifts and who call us all to live justly and to worship the God of Love" (A. J. Han Van den Blink, Regional Chair).

19

My Discernment of Spirits

Still believing that I was free to speak to Dignity on topics other than homosexuality, I signed up to give a workshop on spirituality at the Seattle convention in 1983, the same convention at which Archbishop Hunthausen got into trouble when he invited Dignity to celebrate at his cathedral. Just prior to the convention, I broke my ankle in an accident on the Olympic Peninsula during a preconvention vacation with Charlie and was unable to give my workshop. When I arrived back in New York, I received a call from my provincial, who told me that Apostolic Delegate Pio Laghi, in Washington, D.C., was on the phone. He said he had a copy of the Dignity convention program and wanted to know if I gave the workshop listed, so he could report it to Rome. I think it was providential that I had had my accident. Had I spoken, I think I would have been dismissed from the Jesuits immediately. Because I had not spoken, I had two more years to continue my work as a Jesuit and prepare myself for my expulsion.

The final series of events that led to my expulsion from the Jesuits and my freedom to publish and speak again in the media began with the Dignity convention in New York City in August 1985. This was the seventh biennial convention and the seventh at which I was invited to speak. I gave a talk entitled "New Dimensions of Christian Freedom," in which I dealt with such topics as the freedom to be "born again," the freedom to play, freedom of conscience, and the role of human freedom at the moment of death. I was very careful to abide by the guidelines that I had received from the Vatican, as I understood them, so I did not address the issue of homosexuality directly. For close to ten years, I had been walking a difficult path between the impersonal and, as they appeared to me, insensitive directives I had received from Rome and the sufferings and needs of the lesbians and gay men whom God had called me to serve. I had done the best I could to uphold the responsibility I owed to the church as well as the responsibility I owed to my gay brothers and lesbian sisters. Never once in those ten years did anyone from Rome involved in the decisions that directly affected my ministry and life enter into direct dialogue with me.

In November 1985, two months after the convention, I was called in by my provincial, Father Joseph Novak, and informed that because of complaints from the local hierarchy, Cardinal Ratzinger of the CDF had called the General of the Society of Jesus and given him an order, which he was to pass on to me. I was to "withdraw from any and all ministry to homosexual persons." Father General Peter Hans Kolvenbach expressed a willingness to allow me to continue my private ministry of psychotherapy, for which he expressed "a sincere respect and value." However, he absolutely forbade me to take part in any way in public ministry to gay people. I was not to be associated in any way with homosexual causes, including passive attendance at a meeting or liturgy. (I joked at the time that that would prevent me from attending any Jesuit community meeting or liturgy.) He also made it clear that if my private ministry of psychotherapy came to public attention, he could not guarantee that the congregation would agree to allow me to continue even that. The provincial asked me to spend some time in prayer and discernment before I answered.

To try to discern what God wanted me to do, I spent several months in prayer and consultation with spiritual advisors. There were two key moments that helped me reach a decision during those difficult months of discernment. The first was the advice of a former Jesuit provincial and spiritual guide, Father Joe Towle. After I described to him all the pros and cons I had been debating, he suggested to me that I was going about the discernment process all wrong. I was still too much "in my head." He told me that if he went outside his residence in the South Bronx and saw someone lying at the curb, asked what was wrong, and was told the person had no food and no bed to sleep in, then he knew what God was asking of him—to find food and shelter for this poor human being. Because of my gayness and my pastoral experience, God had put me in touch, on both personal and pastoral levels, with the special pain and suffering of gay people. Then it was perfectly clear that God was calling me to relieve those sufferings in any way I could, regardless of the consequences.

My advisor also recalled for me the meditation all Jesuits make on what

Ignatius called "the three degrees of humility." Ignatius saw these as three steps into a closer identity and intimacy with Jesus: "Humility lies in the acceptance of Jesus Christ as the fullness of what it means to be human." Ignatius is echoing the words of Paul that we are all called to form the perfect human "until all of us come . . . to maturity, to the measure of the full stature of Christ" (Ephesians 4:13). Ignatius continues:

> To be humble is to live as close to the truth as possible: that I am created in the likeness of Christ, that I am meant to live according to the pattern of his paschal mystery, and that my whole fulfillment is to be found in being next to Christ as he draws me to himself.

In the first degree of humility, Ignatius suggests that I ask God's grace to never consider any action that would separate me from God and Jesus, even if my life depended on it.

> I would do nothing that would cut me off from God—not even if I were made head of all creation or even just to save my own life here on earth. I know that grave sin in this sense is to miss the whole meaning of being a person—one who is created and redeemed and is destined to live forever in love with God, my creator and Lord.

The second degree is to seek the grace to be indifferent to a long life or a short one, to honors or to disgrace, to pleasure or to suffering, in order to be free to do whatever Jesus wants of me.

> My life is firmly grounded in the fact that the reality of being a person is seen fully in Jesus Christ. Just as "I have come to do your will, oh God" is the motivating force of his life, so the only real principle of choice in my life is to seek out and do the will of the Father. With this habitual attitude, I find I can maintain a certain balance in my inclination to have riches rather than poverty, honor rather than dishonor, or to desire a long life rather than a short one. I would not want to turn away from God even in small ways, because my whole desire is to respond ever more faithfully to his call.

The third degree is most perfect humility, namely:

> In order to imitate and be more actually like Christ our Lord, I want and choose poverty with Christ poor rather than riches, opprobrium with Christ replete with it rather than honors, and to desire to be rated as worthless and a fool for Christ, Who first was held as such, rather than wise and prudent in this world.

In a note, Ignatius acknowledges that this third degree is a special grace, a gift that comes primarily from God's initiative. He recommends, at this point, that one return in prayer to the colloquy which reads:

First, I approach Our Lady, asking her to obtain for me from her Son the grace-gift to follow him in the highest spiritual poverty, and should God be pleased thereby and want to choose and accept me, even in actual poverty. Even greater is the gift I seek in being able to bear the insults and contempt of the world, so imitating Christ, my Lord, ever more closely.

The Spiritual Exercises of Saint Ignatius Loyola

David Fleming, S.J., has reworded the third degree as follows:

I so much want the truth of Christ's life to be the truth of my own that I find myself, moved by grace, with a love and a desire for poverty in order to be with the poor Christ; a love and desire for insults in order to be closer to Christ in his rejection by people; a love and a desire to be considered worthless and a fool for Christ, rather than be esteemed as wise and prudent according to the standards of this world. By grace, I find myself so moved to follow Jesus Christ in the most intimate union possible, that his experiences are reflected in my own. In that I find my delight.

The Spiritual Exercises of Saint Ignatius Loyola: A Literal Translation and a Contemporary Reading (St. Louis: The Institute of Jesuit Resources, 1978)

As a young man in novitiate at St. Andrew on Hudson, I vividly remember my very strong reaction to this third degree. I felt strongly that I was not ready to go that far. I realize now that the strength of my reaction was based in the fact that I was still relating primarily to a god of fear. When I read the words of John in Revelation: "Amen. Come, Lord Jesus!" (22:20), I spontaneously prayed, "Wait, Lord Jesus, wait!" I was not ready for the kind of intimacy Ignatius sought because I was not yet open to such a deep and radical loving intimacy with my God. Still, I followed Ignatius's advice and made the triple colloquy, praying to Mary, her son Jesus, and the Father that someday, when I was ready, to grant me the grace to grow into and experience that kind of passionate desire for the deepest possible union and intimacy with the Lord. Little did I know that my decision in conscience to continue my ministry to lesbians and gays would become the occasion for me to receive an answer to that young novice's prayers and to have a very real and joyful experience of the third degree of humility.

The second moment that helped me reach my decision occurred while I spent a week at the Trappist monastery, Gethsemane, in Kentucky. One day in holy week while I was in prayer, agonizing over the decision that was due that weekend, a knock came at the door of my room, and a monk with a great red beard, whom I did not know and had never seen before, handed me a slip of paper. On that paper was written the Buddhist vow of compassion, the Bodhisattva's Vow of Universal Redemption. He explained to me that a bodhisattva is one who, after attaining enlightenment, defers entrance into nirvana—that is, the cessation of the cycle of birth and death—and chooses instead to continue being born in a human body in order to share the burden of others' sufferings and sorrows and to aid them with compassionate presence. Sharing the suffering of the human race, the bodhisattva freely chooses "exile" until all human beings can enter into salvation. The vow reads:

> I take upon myself the burden of my suffering brothers (and sisters). I am resolved to do so. I will endure it. I will not turn or run away. I will not turn back. I cannot.
>
> And Why? My endeavors do not merely aim at my own deliverance. I must help all my brothers (and sisters). May I be a balm to those who are sick, their healer and servant until sickness come never again. May I become an unfailing store for my poor brothers (and sisters) and serve them in their need. May I be in the famine at the ages' end, their drink and their meat.
>
> My own being, all my life, all my spirituality in the past, present and future I surrender that my brothers (and sisters) may win through to their end, for they dwell in my spirit.
>
> Geske Namgyal Wangchen, *Awakening the Mind of Enlightenment: Meditations on the Buddhist Path* (Boston: Wisdom Publication, 1987)

The spirit of this vow is exactly the spirit being lived out by thousands of gay and lesbian people as well as many others who have dedicated themselves as volunteers to do whatever they can to relieve the suffering of persons with AIDS. I was struck by the statement that actor Anthony Perkins made just a few days before his death from AIDS (*New York Times*, September 14, 1992):

> There are many that believe that this disease is God's vengeance, but I believe it was sent to teach people how to love and understand and have compassion for each other. I have learned more about love, selflessness and human understanding from the people I have met in this great adventure in the world of AIDS than I ever did in the cutthroat, competitive world in which I spent my life.

The Buddhist vow brought back to mind the spiritual meaning of Christ's life, the quality of compassion, expressed in one of my favorite texts in scripture:

> Let the same mind be in you that was in Christ Jesus, who, though he was in the form of God, did not regard equality with God as something to be exploited, but emptied himself, taking the form of a slave, being born in human likeness. And being found in human form, he humbled himself and became obedient to the point of death—even death on a cross.
>
> Therefore God also highly exalted him and gave him the name that is above every name, so that at the name of Jesus every knee should bend, in heaven and on earth and under the earth, and every tongue should confess that Jesus Christ is Lord, to the glory of God the Father. (Philippians 2:5–11)

Whenever I prayed over the possibility of obeying the order I received from Rome to give up all ministry to lesbians and gays, my spirit was troubled, and I had a strong feeling that I did not have the right in conscience to abandon the gay community that had turned to me for help and guidance. In the course of my nearly ten years of silence in obedience to the Vatican, my understanding of how to discern the will of God changed, I hope, for the better. It had grown and matured under the constant pressure of trying to do God's will within the confines of restrictive directives from Rome.

Roman authorities were inclined to see my efforts to interpret their restrictions on my freedom in the narrowest of possible ways as revealing too "legalistic" an attitude and as playing games with obedience. I saw my effort as an honest attempt to try to put together my obedience to the orders I received from Rome with my obedience to the will of God, calling me to a ministry of compassion to gay people. I kept in mind a legal principle of interpretation of canon law: *Odiosa sint restringenda* ("Restrictive laws are to be most narrowly interpreted").

As Eduard Schillebeeckx, a Dutch Catholic theologian, observes in *Ministry: Leadership in the Community of Jesus Christ* (New York: Crossroad, 1981),

> Christian obedience is also listening so as to be involved in the kairos of the moment of grace of a particular time, listening in obedience to the sufferings of human beings and the seeds of a Christian community, and then performing specific actions in conformity with "that voice of God." This is also and above all a fundamental form of Christian obedience, derived from the authority of human beings who are suffering and in need.

Schillebeeckx goes on to observe that when this form of obedience comes into conflict with authority, Thomas Aquinas allows that a human conscience that has been tested in such a conflict (and not just because it is sure of itself) is free to make a decision contrary to authority and, moreover, adds that a conscientious person must do this "even if he knows that as a result he can be excommunicated by the Church."

God had granted me that grace, an intimate awareness of the sufferings and seeds of community among my lesbian sisters and gay brothers. First of all, I knew my own sufferings as a gay man and a gay priest. My struggles to reconcile my faith and trust in God with my self-acceptance and my ministry to gay people, including my work as psychotherapist with hundreds of gay clients, had put me in intimate contact with the special psychological pain most gay people suffer in our culture and especially in the Catholic church. I became intensely aware that, unless we are dealing with a sadistic god, what is so destructive psychologically for so many people has to be bad theology.

There was great suffering not only for individual men and women but also for the gay community at large. The massive crucifixion by AIDS has rivaled in its virulence any plague of the Middle Ages. I understood that the special gifts—gifts of understanding, self-acceptance as a gay man, and trust in God's love and mercy—that God has given me were there so that I could share them with others like myself. I could become an instrument of God's compassion.

Although I was leaning toward deciding to disobey the Vatican order, I was aware that my decision might be wrong, that subtle forms of egoism and self-deceit might be influencing it. I was also aware, however, that fear and the urge to be secure within the church and the Jesuit order should not deter me from bearing witness from within the church to what I thought and felt was the truth. I had to trust that, if I were wrong, God would make my error known to me and the Holy Spirit would protect those whom my error might endanger. If my decision was right, good consequences would flow from it into the lives of those to whom I ministered.

I have frequently preached to my gay family that we must be prepared to "embrace ourselves as exiles." We must be prepared to accept our exile state both within society and in the church. We must grieve and gradually let go of the desire to "belong" to all the institutions of this world. We must deepen our spiritual roots and our realization that, in direct proportion to our exile status in this world, we belong in a deeper and more cosmic level to a community bound together by God's love and God's mercy. I know that the decision to continue my public ministry would require me to learn to practice what I had been preaching on an even more profound level.

Finally, it was clear to me what my decision must be. I wrote to my religious superiors in 1985: "God has called me to a ministry of compassion to gay people and I cannot in conscience renounce that ministry."

That refusal to obey the Vatican's latest order brought with it a rather surprising grace of real peace and joy. I had struggled for nine years to discern whether my silence was following the will of God according to my vows as a Jesuit or whether it was, instead, cowardice and fear of the consequences of disobedience. I also continued to be uncertain that my decision to speak out and disobey was not influenced by some subtle form of egoism and a desire to be in the limelight. But I hoped and prayed that God was calling me to speak out and accept the consequences of being separated from my religious family and from my legal right to exercise my priesthood. I believed that this was my personal call to the "third degree of humility." I became convinced that gay people needed a spokesperson and defender in the Catholic church who, from personal experience, could fearlessly speak the truth about gayness.

I brought my decision once more before God for a final discernment during a retreat at Mount Savior Monastery near Elmira, New York. During prayer I had the distinct impression that God was annoyed with me for badgering God for further evidence. The answer I seemed to get from God was "Leave me alone; I don't care what you do. You choose and I will go along with you down whatever path you choose!" I remember praying excitedly, "If that is so, God, I have no doubt what I would like to choose." Again, the answer I got was "Go ahead, choose, and I will go with you!" God is certainly full of surprises. I ended my letter to my provincial, telling him of my decision to disobey the order, with these words:

> I know that the imminent possibility of my separation from the Society of Jesus and from the official priesthood has caused me intense grief and sorrow; this has been my central identity for the last forty years. Yet God in her mercy has granted me some consolation. I feel sure that God's mysterious providence is guiding all our deliberations, even if their conclusions are momentarily in con-

flict. Someday we will both look back in joy and wonder on how God's love achieved its goal both because of and despite all of us.

Please keep me and my ministry to the gay community in your prayers, Joe, and I will continue to pray for you and the Society which I love. In obedience to the will of God as I understand it, I remain sincerely yours,

John J. McNeill

I was particularly grateful for the support I continued to receive from my Jesuit Community at Ninety-eighth Street, with whom I continued the process of communal discernment. When they heard that I was threatened with dismissal from the Jesuits if I did not give up my ministry, they sent the following letter, composed by Dan Berrigan, to the General Peter Hans Kolvenbach:

Dear Father General,

We are writing you with regard to your proximate meeting in New York, with John McNeill of our community.

We are concerned about the treatment John has received during the past years from officials in the Church. We are deeply disturbed by the impasse which has developed regarding his future in the Society.

We are also witnessing current Roman practice, as it touches on the American church. We see the treatment accorded our bishops and theologians, the scrutinizing of seminaries and universities, all of which seems of one piece with the McNeill crisis. Authorities have evidently determined that the era of Vatican II is ended; that bishops (especially those we Jesuits most emulate) are to be strictly surveilled, and when deemed necessary, removed; that the sensus fidelium is to be ignored; that theological investigation is dangerous and unacceptable.

We cannot breathe in such an atmosphere. As Jesuits, we are appalled that the Church we love, and indeed are vowed to serve is threatening, stifling, ostracizing its best daughters and sons, those whom we have been urged to emulate, those graciously endowed with intelligence and courage.

We wonder what is to become of the Society, if voices prevail which seem for the present to gain the most attentive hearing in Rome.

We think it honorably due our brother Jesuits, that superiors defend and protect our members. We see no virtue in an obedience that simply submits, when a Jesuit is ordered to abandon his work under pain of dismissal. We see nothing authentically Ignatian in bowing before such treatment, indeed we suspect submission would fall under the canon of sinfulness.

On the occasion of your visit to the United States, we wish to put on record our loving respect for Fr. McNeill, our gratitude for his courage. In his retreats and public lectures and counseling, he has merited well of the Society and the Church, succoring a despised, alienated and afflicted community. In his careful scholarly writing he has given attention to a question, certainly disputed, but just as certainly crucial, both from a moral and human point of view.

Is silencing Fr. McNeill, or worse, dismissing him from our Society, likely to serve the cause of truth? Does not such a course rather raise the suspicion that the Church fears the truth, and therefore chooses to punish a Jesuit who pursues it?

If McNeill is to be made an example of, we have an ominous sense that he will by no means be the last. We wonder who next will feel the punishing hand of authority, destroying his work, assaulting his good name and status in the Society.

We believe that if John McNeill is dismissed, we lose more than an outstanding Jesuit; there is another, no less serious, consequence. Others will read the by no means mysterious handwriting on the wall, the clear sign that theological discussion, controversial areas of ministry, forms of authority that consult the faithful, and perhaps most of all, intellectual courage—that these are no longer valued in the Society. Jesuits, among others, will be well advised to play life safe, to stay within narrow human and theological bounds, to accept cultural stereotypes of who is acceptable and who objectionable (the former of whom alone we are free to serve).

By so reacting, Jesuits will fall into the worst racist and sexist stereotypes of our culture. Among those must be included current attitudes toward the homosexual community, and those who minister there. We are appalled that some American church officials have sanctioned the worst public attitudes toward our gay sisters and brothers, including those in the Christian community. Indeed, "sanctioned" does not describe the intensity of the crusade against gay men and women, local church campaigns against gay rights legislation, denial of the sacraments, persecution of priests who minister to gays.

And now, the McNeill case; its bizarre course and impending conclusion.

We wonder. We wonder why Fr. McNeill has been singled out for condign punishment. We wonder what institutions or interests are being served by his dismissal. We wonder why the gay community has been singled out, as undeserving of Jesuit ministry, beyond the pale of our compassion—among all the minorities of the world, all the debatable, controversial ministries of the church.

We wonder why the church has not singled out those who minister say, to juntas, generals, admirals, crime syndicates, shady politicians and bankers, millionaire oppressors of the poor, nuclear weapons engineers, highly placed employees of pentagons, kremlins. We wonder why those who offer communion to Pinochet or Marcos are not singled out. We wonder why those Catholics who presently deride and denounce the noblest of our bishops are not singled out.

We believe that the McNeill case is a watershed for the Society. In the long haul, as history comes to bear on us, we Jesuits are being urged in two directions. The first is the continuity of our tradition, which urges us to prefer the poor, to take our place with the despised and outcast, to abominate repression, control of minds and hearts. The second is the present lamentable course of things; the canceling out of the generosity and breadth of Vatican II, the obsession with order, unquestioning obedience, servility of spirit.

We pray that the Society will stand in courage with those of our brothers whose lives are placed in question and whose work is threatened. No one can harm the Society more grievously than we harm ourselves. If we submit before the safe middle way in church and world, we perforce abandon our best and dearest brothers, who have chosen another, more painful way. But if we stand together, by no means against the church, but in the best and closest evangelical tradition, then surely, among other blessings, we will avoid the death of the heart, the loss of a sense of one another, the sense of who we are in the church and world.

We do not know how else, except by an exemplary courage, the Society will survive the pervasive illness, east and west, of cultures of conformity and control.

We pray for you, in your present difficult office and we pray for Fr. McNeill, our brother.

This letter was signed by eighteen members of the Ninety-eighth Street community. It meant a great deal to me and gave a considerable boost to my morale while I was going through the process of dismissal. These were my Jesuit brothers who had worked beside me day by day and were in the best position to pass judgment on the meaning and quality of my ministry. Father General Kolvenbach assured me that he received this letter from my community and would give it due consideration. Obviously, my brothers did not prevail, but their letter gives me confidence to this day that I was doing the work appropriate to my Jesuit vocation. Shortly after my dismissal, the New York province ordered all Jesuits to cease working with Dignity.

Another source of support for me at that time was a group of Protestant theologians organized by the Reverend Robert Raines at Kirkridge. Among those who wrote to Cardinal Hamer were William Sloane Coffin, James Nelson, Reverend Paul Moore Jr., the Episcopal bishop of New York. Bishop Moore shared a letter he sent to Cardinal Hamer in which he stated that my ministry to gays and lesbians was as important to his church as it was to Roman Catholics.

20

Expulsion

During this process, Charlie was afraid that the hierarchy would order me to go to Rome for some kind of hearing. Because of his Sicilian heritage, Charlie has a very strong distrust of authorities in general and the Italian hierarchy in particular. He wanted me to promise that I would refuse such an order because he suspected the motives of the Roman power structure. Charlie was afraid I might disappear into some underground dungeon in Castle Sant'Angelo, never to be seen alive again. Consequently, I was fearful that I might receive an order to report to Rome that I would feel obliged to obey. So, to my great relief, on October 19, 1986, Father General Peter Hans Kolvenbach held a two-hour meeting with me at Fordham University in the Bronx. Charlie was parked outside with the motor running so he could provide a quick getaway, if needed.

At that meeting the General made it clear to me that my public ministry to gay people was not compatible with the mission of the Society of Jesus. What I understood by that was that my ministry would come into conflict with the Jesuit special fourth vow of direct obedience to the Roman pontiff. Consequently, if I made the decision to continue in that ministry, he would be obliged to expel me from the Society of Jesus.

I made it clear to him from my side that I felt obliged in conscience to continue that ministry. The General assured me that my expulsion would not be a judgment on my ministry; mine would be an "honorable discharge." He mentioned that Mother Teresa was expelled from her teaching order because her work with the poor and the homeless in the streets of Calcutta was not compatible with the teaching mission of her order, the Sisters of Notre Dame de Namur. The General shared with me his grief at being separated from the

Arab Christian community in Lebanon, where he had served as a missionary for many years. I gave the General a copy of an article I had prepared for the *Christian Century*, "The Church Should Be a Home for All People." He told me he would read the article on his flight to South America. He warned me not to show the article to my provincial because he would be obliged to dismiss me immediately. The article was subsequently published in the March 11, 1987, issue. He ended by asking for my blessing and giving me his. I left that meeting filled with a joyful spirit and gratitude to God.

The final event that precipitated my choice to renew my public ministry was the Vatican "Halloween" letter on homosexuality issued on October 31, 1986. I see the providence of God in that letter. Its homophobic spirit, in total contradiction to the spirit of the Gospels, is so obvious that no one living out the spirit of Christ can grant it any credibility and authority. I believe that it has actually helped gay Catholics and other Christians to mature, stop depending on outside authority, and take charge of their own liberation. To quote a famous liberation theologian:

> Liberation from oppression is a true value of the gospel. We must become aware that Christian freedom comes from within through the Spirit of Christ and we must become aware that freedom is something to be claimed, not granted from without. We must listen to the spirit within us, listen to the voices of the oppressed around us and then, act for human rights and equality.

The congregation's letter went far beyond any legitimate affirmation of religious or moral concern about homosexual activity. When it asserts that homosexual orientation is an "objective disorder" without taking into account all the scientific evidence that casts doubt on that opinion, when it accuses all of us who seek civil justice for gay people as being "callous" to the risk of the lives of our gay brothers and sisters because of the AIDS crisis, and, finally, when it lays blame for the "irrational and violent reactions" of homophobes on the victims of the violence because they have the effrontery to seek justice and their civil rights, the Vatican exhibits a mean and cruel spirit that is in essential conflict with both the spirit and the letter of the Gospels. The Vatican hierarchy seems convinced that all they have to do is assert something as true, and that makes it true. I could not continue my silence in the face of that evil.

On All Souls' Day, November 2, 1986, I issued a press release in response
to that letter, breaking my nine-year silence. The process of my dismissal from
the Jesuits was thus set in motion. My provincial immediately issued an order
of separation and applied to the Congregation for Religious in Rome for a decree of dismissal. Father General refused to be the instrument of my dismissal
from the Jesuits and, instead, turned over my case to Cardinal Hamer of the
Congregation for Religious.

When the decree arrived, I issued the following press release:

> After thirty-eight wonderful years as a Jesuit priest, I was informed Wednesday,
> 28th January 1987, that I have been dismissed from the Jesuit order by a decree
> issued by Jerome Hamer, Cardinal prefect for the Vatican Congregation for Re-
> ligious.
>
> The grounds for my dismissal was my public dissent from the Church's teach-
> ing on homosexuality. The Vatican perceives that dissent as causing grave scan-
> dal, as injurious to the teaching authority of the Church and potentially as
> injurious to the salvation of souls.
>
> I was given ten days to seek a revocation of the decree. To help me present
> evidence to the Vatican that the charges against me are not true, I am calling
> on all those who read my book, *The Church and the Homosexual*, and/or those
> who have been influenced by my ministry to write to Jerome Cardinal Hamer,
> O.P., prefect for the Congregation for Religious, and give witness to the influ-
> ence my writing and/or my ministry has had on their faith and their relation-
> ship with the Church.
>
> I do not have great hope that the decree will be recalled. However, I am still
> a priest and a loyal Catholic. I will continue my ministry to gay people through
> writing, speaking and psychotherapy to the best of my ability. And I shall al-
> ways be a Jesuit in spirit and feel a special bond of love and respect for the So-
> ciety of Jesus.

Since my decision to speak out, I have received hundreds of letters, many
from clergy and religious, who have given witness to the rightness of my decision. Many acknowledged that their return to the practice of their faith or
their priestly or religious vocation was due to my writings and ministry. My Jesuit Community at Ninety-eighth Street issued a press release, deploring the
decision to dismiss me from the order and expressing their admiration for my
work and their continued solidarity with me.

The final decree of dismissal was issued on April 13, 1987. In it, Cardinal
Hamer acknowledged the receipt of hundreds of letters from gay people,

attesting to the benefits that have come to them through you. Their testimony does not, however, alter the facts on which this dismissal is based. Neither they nor you have denied those facts. Certainly we are aware of your deep concern for the problems and the sufferings of homosexual men and women and of your desire to alleviate that pain. However, we regret that you have sought and continue to seek remedies and solutions which are not in keeping with the authentic teaching of the Church and are, in fact, contradictory to that teaching. The Church has tried in various ways to respond to the real anguish and pain of persons of homosexual orientation. But solutions which deny the clear and constant teaching of the Church or hold out an unreasonable expectation of change in that teaching can create an illusory relief and an even greater pain and frustration.

The cardinal's letter made clear that Rome placed ideology before pastoral concern. The cardinal reaffirmed the decree of dismissal and closed off all avenues of appeal.

On Apri 14, 1987, the Jesuit provincial, Fr. Joseph Novak, S.J., and his assistant, the vice-provincial, came to my apartment on Riverside Drive to officially promulgate the decree of expulsion. Two witnesses from the Ninety-eighth Street Jesuit Community were present, my friend and spiritual director, Fr. Robert Springer, S.J., and Fr. David Toolan, S.J. The provincial was strictly business, reading the decrees of dismissal and *exclaustration* in Latin and English. Through my tears, I remember begging the provincial to continue a ministry to gays and lesbians in the New York province, a request that went unheeded. I and the witnesses signed the decrees, and my expulsion was brought to a close.

Shortly after my dismissal, Walter Wink, the biblical theologian, wrote me these prophetic words: "John, when the Vatican imprudently slammed the door on you, the gust of wind it set off blew open hundreds of doors. In the craftiness of God, I swear, your impact will be increased exponentially." Indeed, in May of 1995, Robert D. McCleary, a student at Weston Jesuit School of Theology, presented a thesis to his director, Roger Haight, S.J. He chose as the topic of his research thesis "The Expulsion of John McNeill: An Event at the Intersection of the Ordinary Magisterium, the Society of Jesus, Sexual Ethics, and Pastoral Praxis." Robert McCleary asked a series of questions which he proposed to answer:

> Was McNeill's ministry to gays and lesbians an ethically sound one? Did the way he was treated by the CDF and the Society of Jesus lack ethical merit? Does

Scripture provide a grounding for the ministry of John McNeill? How does the "fourth vow" of direct obedience to the Pope impact on this case? Can it be shown that McNeill himself acted ethically by personally following conscience rather than obedience? What was the purpose and net effect of silencing legitimate dissent? Who if anyone gave scandal in this case, McNeill or the magisterium? Was the entire handling of this matter by the magisterium and by the Society of Jesus unacceptable in terms of the models of consultation, reconciliation and openness defined and embraced by the Second Vatican Council?

With these questions forming the facets of his investigation, McCleary states that the problem in this case can be encapsulated by the question, "Should the Society of Jesus have expelled John J. McNeill?" After examining all the pertinent documents, McCleary came to this conclusion concerning the ethical value of my ministry to gays and lesbians: "The ministry of John McNeill was a mission in the long-standing Jesuit tradition, especially as that mission was reformulated in the documents of the 32nd General Congregation."

McCleary concludes that the judgment on the ethical validity of my ministry must then be in the affirmative.

> Given the identity of the gay and lesbian community as marginalized and suffering, it is a community of the type to which Jesus himself was attracted. Given the fact that a primary aim of this ministry is the reconciliation of an alienated group to God and the Church, it is worthy of the Church's support. Given the fact that another main goal of the ministry is the encouragement of a dialogue for the greater mutual education and understanding of the gay and lesbian community and the Church, it is worthy of widespread participation. Given that the underpinning of this ministry is a positive theology and a vibrant spirituality, which has grown out of the overlapping of the Word of God, tradition and the personal experiences of gay and lesbian Christians, it is wholly of a piece with the Gospel message of Christ.

Examining all the scriptural issues, McCleary concludes:

> While the scriptural basis for condemnation of homosexuality is in sufficient doubt as to be non-compelling, scriptural support for ministry to the disenfranchised is prominent and powerfully impelling. . . .
>
> The Society of Jesus would be a much stronger body, with a redoubled sense of purpose and identity in mission to the world, had it ridden out the storm and stood by John McNeill until persons of position and power in the hierarchy of

the Church began to make public statements like this of Cardinal Hume: *Love between two persons, whether of the same sex or a different sex, is to be treasured and respected. . . . To love another is in fact to reach out to God, who shares his lovableness with the one we love. To be loved is to receive a sign or share in God's unconditional love. To love another, whether of the same sex or a different sex, is to have entered the area of the richest human experience.*

When I first read this critique of the society by McCleary, my first impulse was to come to the defense of the Jesuits. I realized on an ever deeper level how much the need to keep the society good and make myself the bad one had controlled my thinking and feeling all through the process of my dismissal. And, of course, I was a gay man in an "illicit" relationship that contradicted my vows. I never imagined that the Jesuits should have given me total support in my ministry. In fact, I spent most of my time hiding from their observation. Consequently, I am grateful to Robert McCleary for opening my eyes to what should have been the ideal relationship between me and my Jesuit superiors and for showing me that my dismissal had more to do with the problems of Jesuit superiors both in New York and in Rome than with any fault on my part

Finally, it is important to establish what my dismissal from the Society of Jesus did and did not involve in my relationship with the church. Frequently, I hear myself referred to in the media as an "ex-priest." This is not true. I am still a priest in the Roman Catholic Church in good standing. To legally exercise my priesthood in the public arena, I would need to seek *incardination* into a diocese. I have not sought to be accepted in any diocese for three reasons. First, any diocese that accepted me would want me to move to that diocese and give up my ministry and psychotherapeutic practice in New York City. Second, I believe that any bishop willing to accept me in his diocese would have to apply the same conditions that the Vatican applied by ordering me to give up all ministry to gays and lesbians. Third, my now out-of-the-closet relationship with Charlie would prevent my being accepted; the church has not yet reached the maturity where it can acknowledge the compatibility of a loving human sexual relationship with the pastoral priestly service of God.

21

Where Will I Be Buried?

A year after my dismissal, I returned to Mount Savior Monastery for my annual retreat. I anticipated a quiet retreat, during which I would express my gratitude to God, untroubled any further by my need to discern spirits. To my surprise, I no sooner placed myself in the presence of God and began to pray when an unexpected question popped into my mind: Where will I be buried? This is typically an Irish question. For some reason, death and the last things have always been of primary concern to the Irish. I still remember that the greatest compliment the Irish priest of my childhood could pay was to wish you a large funeral. Every morning, I open my *New York Times* first to the obituary page, the "Irish scratch sheet," I like to call it, and pray for those departed souls.

If I were still a member of the Jesuit order, I would be buried in the Jesuit graveyard of the New York Province at the Shrine of the North American Martyrs in Auriesville, New York. While still a member, I used to go there, estimate where I would be buried, lie down on the ground, and get the feel of it. I thought that there could be no better place and no better companions with whom to greet the resurrection.

It dawned on me as I prayed that I was expelled not only from the order but also from the order's graveyard. Tears welled in my eyes as that realization came to me, and I began to mourn my separation from the Jesuits in a new and deeper way. "Well, God," I prayed, "You really have no mercy on a gay man! Not only are we exiles in this world, we are exiles even in death!" I went through the deepest and most painful experience of mourning at that time. That evening I called my family in Buffalo to see if there was any room for me in the family plot. There wasn't. The next morning I visited the public graveyard at the monastery. There was a delightful statue of Jesus as an adolescent bringing home the lost sheep. Jesus and the sheep both had big smiles on their faces. I decided then and there to ask permission from the abbot, Father Martin, to be buried there, but the Abbot informed me with sorrow that the cemetery was "oversubscribed."

I then considered cremation, so I called Charlie and asked him, "If I were cremated and left you my ashes, what would you do with them?" After a brief pause, Charlie replied, "I'd put your ashes in the trunk of my car." Surprised, I asked him "Why?" My lover and companion of the last thirty-two years said that if he ever got stuck on the ice he would ask me for one last favor. Once again Charlie's sense of humor was a good tonic for me.

I returned once again to prayer and suddenly I was given a vision of my tombstone:

> Here Lies a Gay Priest
> Who Took a Chance on God!
> John J. McNeill 1925–?

The image of that gravestone filled me with feelings of peace and joy. I could have the last word etched in stone, so to speak. I could preach my message from the grave. Then the question arose: Where could I put that stone? After another period of prayer, I realized that the perfect place would be the memorial garden at Kirkridge Retreat Center, where the ashes of those who have died of AIDS can be scattered. I had given retreats for gays and lesbians at Kirkridge for twenty-two years, frequently twice a year. That made it a perfect spot for my "last word" to be spoken. The trustees at Kirkridge have agreed to my request. With that arrangement, my Irish heart was at peace.

22

Our Home in the Country

Dismissal from the Jesuits at the age of sixty-two was a financial disaster for me. As a form of settlement, the Society of Jesus did give me a small sum of money. However, after nearly forty years of service, with no money in the bank, no investment in Social Security, no savings, and no health insurance, all I had going for me was my therapeutic practice. If my health were to fail me, I faced personal destitution. Of course, Charlie would do his best to support us both, but if he died, the laws are such that I could not receive his pension income. In God's providence, however, something akin to a miracle happened. The apartment I was renting at Ninety-eighth Street and Riverside Drive went co-op shortly after my dismissal from the Jesuits. I was able, with a bank loan, to buy it as an insider and shortly after sell it at a considerable profit. I interpreted this financial windfall as a sign of God's approval of my decision.

Many years before, Charlie decided that we needed to get away from the city and have a quiet place for tranquillity, privacy, prayer, and writing—a country retreat. So he found and bought an old dilapidated cabin on Starlight Lake in Pennsylvania, a few miles from Hancock, New York. Every weekend we could get away, we escaped from the city and spent the weekend in the peace and quiet of our cabin. Charlie repaired and winterized it; we went there year-round, experiencing the dramatic changes of the seasons. We became close friends with Jack and Judy McMahon, who own and operate the Inn at Starlight Lake, and their four children. Jack is a former crooner with the "big bands" and Judy is a former Broadway actress who brought Starlight Theater into existence. They received Charlie and me into their family in a warm and affirming way and have been among our best friends for more than fifteen years. In winter, we parked our car at the inn and skied across the frozen Starlight Lake, dragging our supplies and two cats behind us on a toboggan. Over our years of friendship, we have had the delight of watching the four McMahon children grow up to become wonderful and mature adults.

After the sale of our apartment in New York City, our financial advisors told us that we would lose more than half our profits in taxes unless we rein-vested the money from the sale of our apartment in a new house. The cost of that house would have to equal the sale price of our apartment. After five years of residence, we could then sell the house and keep a certain part of the profit tax free.

Charlie and I searched for a suitable property and decided on a tract of land near Deposit, New York, adjacent to a wildlife preserve, a state forest, and a resort golf course. With the help of an architect friend, we designed our dream home, a contemporary house with a twenty-eight-foot-high cathedral ceiling in the living room, large windows looking out on magnificent views in every direction, a fieldstone fireplace, and a stocked pond as well as a gazebo. Wildlife—deer, wild turkeys, bear—abounds on the grounds. We intended to live there for five years and then sell the house, at which time I expected to be ready to retire.

We moved in, appropriately, during Thanksgiving week of 1989. A year later, Charlie suffered a series of severe heart attacks. In 1991, he underwent quadruple bypass surgery and retired from his work with the Defense Logistics Agency. He stayed permanently at our home in Deposit, while I spent three days a week in New York City for my therapeutic practice. Charlie had a sec-ond bout of severe heart attacks in January of 1997 that have left him seri-ously disabled. We are grateful for every day God gives us to be together.

When I was approaching the age of seventy, I was ready to retire from my therapeutic practice and give the time that remains to me to retreats, writing, and contemplative prayer. To do that, we needed to sell the house. We had our property on the market for more than three years, but because of the poor economy then and the degree of downsizing going on in all the major com-panies in the area, we didn't have even a serious nibble in that time. I prayed daily to God to help us sell our house and let our life move on. In the mean-time, we continued to enjoy the beauty, peace, privacy, and tranquillity of our home in the country. My great delight has always been gardening. My work in the flower gardens has a very spiritual quality. I see each flower as a direct revelation of the beauty of God: "I saw his blood upon the rose!"

Finally, in May of 1997 and at only half its value, we signed a contract for the sale of our house and moved back into our cabin at Starlight, Pennsylvania.

All the proceeds from the sale went into paying off debts. If Charlie were to die ahead of me, I would live in poverty. Once again, I would be living out the third degree of humility of Ignatius's spiritual exercises.

23

Taking a Chance on God

My dismissal from the Jesuits freed me once again to speak and write on the issue of homosexuality. I immediately collected the materials from the talks I had given at Kirkridge over the nine years of my silence to integrate them into the text of a new book. That book, which I composed in the cabin at Starlight Lake, was published in 1988 as *Taking a Chance on God: Liberating Theology for Gays, Lesbians, and Their Lovers, Families, and Friends*.

The title came to me one night in a dream. Since the forties I had always had an affection for a lovely ballad from the musical *Cabin in the Sky*, "Taking a Chance on Love." Scripture tells us that God is love, and whoever truly loves also knows God. I believe, therefore, that "taking a chance on love" and "taking a chance on God" are at some deep level identical, just as Jesus said that the commandment to love your neighbor is identical to the commandment to love God. I looked up the lyrics of that song and found them surprisingly appropriate to the message of my book:

> Taking a Chance on Love
> I thought love's game was over,
> Lady luck had gone away.
> I laid my cards on the table,
> Unable to play.
> Then I heard good fortune say,
> "They're dealing you a new hand today!"
> Oh, here I go again
> I hear those trumpets blow again,
> All aglow again,
> Taking a chance on love.

Here I slide again,
About to take that ride again,
Starry-eyed again,
Taking a chance on love
I thought the cards were a frame up.
I never would try,
But now I'm taking the game up,
And the ace of hearts is high.
Things are mending now,
I see a rainbow blending now,
We'll have our happy ending now,

Vernon Duke, John Latouche,
and Ted Fetter (EMI Miller Catalog Inc., 1940)

The years of study and teaching of psychodynamics at the Institutes and my own years of analysis prepared me to deal with homosexuality from both spiritual and psychotherapeutic dimensions. Applying the principle that whatever is good theology must also be good psychotherapy, and vice versa, I began the book with the effort to distinguish pathological religion from healthy religion. I located the essence of all pathological religion as basing our relationship with God in fear. Scripture tells us "perfect love casts out fear." It is equally true that perfect fear casts out love. "For you did not receive a spirit of slavery to fall back into fear, but you have received a spirit of adoption. When we cry, 'Abba! Father!' it is that very Spirit bearing witness with our spirit that we are children of God" (Rom. 8:15–16).

The pagans of old frequently worshiped their gods out of fear. For example, the Carthaginians in Jesus' time worshiped Baal. The worship that Baal demanded of them was that every married couple had to throw their firstborn child into a fire in front of Baal. In a recent article in the *New York Times*, archaeologists report having uncovered on the site of the temple of Baal in ancient Carthage a vast number of tiny urns that contain the ashes of the infants sacrificed. If the Carthaginians failed to sacrifice, Baal threatened them with famine, earthquake, plagues, and wars. They worshiped Baal purely out of fear. They did not and could not love Baal; on the contrary, they hated him. But they obeyed. How often I hear television evangelists preach a Christian Baal and base worship of God on fear. Frequently, they urge us gays and lesbians to sacrifice our hope of any life of sexual love and intimacy to this Christian Baal to escape his wrath. Such a service of fear would blaspheme the God of love that Jesus revealed.

My first book, *The Church and the Homosexual*, was written like a lawyer's brief, examining in detail and refuting all the traditional arguments for condemnation of homosexuality in scripture, tradition, and philosophy. I also examined the general misconceptions about human sexual development. In contrast, *Taking a Chance on God* is a very different book—more readable, less technical, and much more personal. It reflects my own lifelong struggle to accept my gayness with gratitude as a gift from God. Because of my years of training and experience as a psychotherapist with hundreds of gay and lesbian clients, I was able to combine insights from psychotherapy and spirituality to help my readers overcome any interiorized homophobia, shame, guilt, and fear that resulted from religious training and cultural and family prejudices. *Taking a Chance on God* is a more explicitly spiritual book. In fact, many of its chapters end in a prayer. I believe that this book opens the door to a new ethical understanding and acceptance of homosexual relationships as morally good, and gay love as a deeper sharing in divine love.

Chapter 16 in the book, "The Relationship between Mary, the Mother of God, and the Gay and Lesbian Community," had an interesting history. I originally did not plan a chapter on Mary. While I was working on the book at the cabin at Starlight, however, August 15, the feast of the Ascension of Mary into heaven, came around. This was the anniversary of the day I first pronounced my vows forty years earlier and the first time that feast had occurred since my dismissal from the Jesuits. I decided to go to mass in my local church in Hancock, New York. When I got there, I discovered that there was no mass that morning; I decided to spend an hour in church in meditation. Suddenly, that whole chapter formulated itself in my mind. After the hour of meditation, I rushed back to my cabin and wrote out that chapter, which I think is one of the best in the book. Since publication, conservatives have frequently confronted me about that chapter, especially its ending prayer, which they are inclined to see as blasphemous: "Hail Mary, Queen of heaven, pray for all us queens here on earth—and all us queers, fags, dykes, fems, fairies, fruits, transvestites, transsexuals, and all sexual exiles. For in many ways we are your special children."

This very serious prayer came from the heart of those of us who are sexual exiles in this world to one who shared that identity as an unwed mother. I had a major battle with my publishers to keep that chapter in the book. They wanted me to drop it because it was too exclusively Catholic and would not appeal, they claimed, to Protestant readers. I insisted that if they dropped that chapter I would find another publisher.

Taking a Chance on God was published in 1988 and very well received. However, it had a very different reception from *The Church and the Homosexual* in the public media. Because it was so explicitly religious, the secular press ignored it completely, and this time there were no invitations to talk shows. The religious press—*America, Commonweal, Christian Century*—refused to review it. The gay press reviewed it extensively and, from what I could gather from readers' letters and reports, the best advertising came from enthusiastic readers who spread awareness of the book by word of mouth. I know that many gay Alcoholics Anonymous groups have adopted the book for group study. Christopher Durang recommended it in a "Summer Reading Survey" in the magazine *American Theatre* (Summer 1998). Hundreds of people have written me to credit this book with having saved their lives and helping them heal their deepest wounds of internalized homophobia. I am grateful that God has used me in this manner. The book has had a brisk sale every year now for ten years.

One of the surprises of *Taking a Chance on God* is how well it has been received by heterosexuals. Although the book was written with lesbians and gay readers in mind, The Reverend Margaret Kornfeld, a very dear friend and valued associate who is heterosexual, predicted that the book would be as useful to most straight readers as it is to gays and lesbians. She has made use of the book herself in classes with seminary students and clergy. On her advice, I enlarged the subtitle to include *"lovers, families, and friends."*

I have received numerous letters from parents of lesbians and gays who told me how helpful the book has been in freeing them from pathological religious beliefs based on fear, helping them to find a faith in the God of love, and, consequently, joyfully enabling them to accept their homosexual children. For example, when Bishop Tom Gumbleton held a series of public hearings in the parishes of the diocese of St. Paul, Tom White, a parishioner, gave witness that "as a result of a talk at Augsburg College, Minnesota, by former Jesuit, John McNeill, he came to recognize the homosexual orientation of his daughter as a 'gift from God'" (*National Catholic Reporter*, Nov. 11, 1994,

p. 4). That recognition allowed him and his wife to integrate his lesbian daughter and her lover deeply into their lives as a family. What a welcome surprise it was to read the Catholic bishops' pastoral letter, "Always Our Children," released in October 1997. I have reason to believe my books have had some influence in bringing about this sensitive pastoral statement from the American bishops that is so dramatically in conflict with the insensitive dogmatic and political statement issued by the CDF. In the words of the bishops' pastoral letter: "All in all, it is essential to recall one basic truth. God loves every person as a unique individual. Sexual identity helps to define the unique persons we are. God does not love someone any less simply because he or she is homosexual."

Perhaps the most unexpected surprise was how well *Taking a Chance on God* was received overseas. It was also published in Portuguese, Italian, French, and German. I was invited to Holland to speak at the University of Nijmegen and at the University of Amsterdam. The French gay group, David and Jonathan, invited me to speak about the book at a national meeting of their organization outside Paris immediately after its publication in the United States in 1988. Because I had not spoken French for more than twenty-five years, I asked for a translator. However, when I got up to speak, I experienced what resembled the "gift of tongues" and spoke close to perfect French for more than an hour, only once needing the translator for a word. As a result of that talk, David and Jonathan published my book in French (*Les Exclus de L'Église: Apprendre à s'Aimer*, Paris: Éditiones Filipacchi, 1993) as their own official text.

In a special preface to the French edition, Jacques Perotti, the chaplain of David and Jonathan, wrote:

> I salute the appearance of this book in French as a special grace that God has given us. I know from experience that this book will help thousands of gays and lesbians to make progress on the road to freedom. I hope also that many bishops, theologians, and men and women involved in the Church in other areas of liberation will read this book and will seek to enter into a dialogue based on truth. Then we can become a community of lively faith and hope which does not exclude anyone.

One of my most ardent supporters in France was Pasteur Joseph Doucé, a Baptist minister originally from Holland. Pasteur Doucé first contacted me in New York shortly after the publication of *The Church and the Homosexual*. He helped me find a French publisher, and his bookstore was the primary outlet for my book in France. He founded and operated a special ministry to the sexually disenfranchised in Paris called Le Centre du Christ Liberateur. Every Sunday, Pasteur Doucé held a service at the center at which he made welcome sexual minorities—gays, lesbians, transsexuals, transvestites, and others. After the worship service, all in attendance were invited to his table for dinner, which was accompanied by hymns and readings from scripture.

Pasteur Doucé lived in severe poverty and was totally committed to his ministry. He was the principal spokesperson on French television for the civil rights of gays and other sexual minorities and was also president of a European association of Gay and Lesbian Religious Groups from all over Europe. In 1989, he invited me to go with him to Strasbourg. Charlie and I went to Paris to meet him. We noticed that he seemed disturbed; he asked us not to come to his church to meet him. While at the meeting in Strasbourg, we gave a joint television interview, during which Joseph argued that the age of consent should be lowered and brought out other civil rights concerns for the new European constitution that was being written in Strasbourg. We met again back in Paris. Joseph and his lover, a man of his own age, invited us to a dinner and a drag show. During dinner, Joseph urged me to give him the right to publish *Taking a Chance on God* in French.

Shortly after Charlie and I returned to New York, we received a call from Pasteur Doucé's lover, telling us that Doucé had disappeared; he feared that he had been kidnapped. He told us that two men who pretended to be police came to Doucé's office at the church and arrested him on charges of pederasty. They said they were taking him to the central police station in Paris. Joseph was missing for four weeks, and the police denied any awareness of his whereabouts. Then his body was found in the Bois de Boulogne with clear evidence that he had been tortured.

As far as I know, no one was ever charged or arrested for the murder of Pasteur Doucé. I am told that members of the secret police openly brag about capturing, torturing, and killing Doucé on the grounds that he was a pederast. In my several years of acquaintance with Pasteur Doucé, I never had any hint that he was a pederast. I believe that he was a genuine loving pastor and friend to all the sexual outcasts and a martyr for the cause of gay liberation. May his soul rest in peace.

24

The Italian Tour

Taking a Chance on God was published in Italian as *Scommettere su Dio: Teologia della Liberazione Omosessuale* (Turin: Edizioni Sonda, 1994). In Italian the title means, literally, "placing a bet on God" as one would bet on a horse race. With his irrepressible sense of humor, Charlie asked our Italian hosts whether they bet win, place, or show. This Italian edition made such an impression that it resulted in the founding of Christian gay and lesbian groups in several of the major cities of Italy. In June 1995, I was invited, with Charlie, to tour Italy speaking to gay groups in Turin, Milan, and Venice. We ended the tour at the Waldensian Protestant Center in Rome for the first national congress of Christian lesbian and gay groups with representatives from all of Italy. For the first time, there were organized Christian gay and lesbian groups throughout Italy prepared to fight for gay rights and reform of church teaching on homosexuality.

While in Rome, I issued a manifesto in the name of Catholic lesbians and gays to the pope and the Vatican. In Italian, its title was *Basta! Basta! Basta!* or "Enough! Enough! Enough!"

As a gay Catholic theologian and psychotherapist, I am fully aware of the enormous destruction recent Vatican documents will cause in the psychic life of young Catholic gays, and of the violence they will provoke against all gay people. I find myself in a dilemma: What kind of faith and trust can I place in a teaching authority that I clearly see acts in an unloving, hateful, and destructive way toward my gay family?

At this point the deliberate ignorance and distortion of homosexuality, the use of "stereotypes and falsehoods" in an official Vatican document, leads us who are gay Catholics to issue the Vatican a serious warning. Your ignorance can no longer be excused as inculpable; it has become of necessity a deliberate and malicious ignorance. In the name of all Catholic gays, and gays and lesbians everywhere, I cry out *Enough!* Enough of your distortions of Scripture that make homosexuals the scapegoats of every disaster! Jesus himself in Luke 10:10 recognized the sin of Sodom as inhospitality to the stranger, yet you support the interpretation of that passage as homosexual activity. Through the centuries you have supported sodomy laws that have sent thousands of gays to their deaths. You continue to claim that a loving homosexual act is condemned in Scripture when competent scholars are nearly unanimous in admitting that nowhere in Scripture is there a clear condemnation of sexual acts between two gay men or lesbians who love each other.

Enough! Enough of your efforts to reduce all homosexual acts to expressions of lust, and of your refusal to see them as potentially expressions of deep, genuine human love! Enough of your efforts to lead young gays to internalize self-hatred with the result that they are able to relate to God only as a god of fear and hate, and lose all hope in a God of love! Enough of your efforts to foster hatred and discrimination against us in the human community! Enough of an ignorance for which there is no excuse. Enough of driving us from the home of our mother, the Church, and denying us the right to the fullness of human love and sexual love! Enough of fostering discrimination against us, even violence and gay-bashing! We cried out to you for bread, you gave us a scorpion instead!

Obviously you could enter into dialogue with the rest of the human community, especially the gay members of that community, to search for the truth under the guidance of the Holy Spirit in the complex issue of homosexuality. But never was there a mandate from Jesus Christ for you to create the truth by fiat! . . .

We gay and lesbian Catholics pray daily that the Holy Spirit will lead you into a spirit of repentance. Just as you apologized to the Jews for supporting anti-Semitism for centuries, so today you must repent and apologize for the centuries of support you have given homophobia. We pray that the Holy Spirit will strengthen you so that you can let go of the hubris that does not allow you to admit past errors. We pray that the Holy Spirit will lead you to search humbly for the truth concerning homosexuality through dialogue with your gay brothers and lesbian sisters.

The only consolation I can offer gays and lesbians in the meantime is a profound hope that the very absurdity and hateful spirit of the Vatican documents will lead lay Catholics to refuse their authority and recognize the contradiction between their message and that of Jesus, who never once spoke a negative word concerning homosexuality.

I work, hope, and pray that lesbian and gay Catholics and other Christians will exercise their legitimate freedom of conscience, discerning what God is saying to them directly through their gay experience. I hope, too, that they will be able to defang the poisons of pathologically homophobic religion, accepting the good news that God loves and accepts them as lesbian and gay and refusing to be caught in the vortex of self-hatred vis-à-vis a god of fear.

25

Support from Metropolitan Community Church

Shortly after my dismissal from the Jesuits, I began to run into problems with Dignity. Although Integrity New York, an Episcopal gay group, had a special celebration in my honor, Dignity New York, which I had helped found, took distance from me. Friends had warned me that, once I lost my identity as a Jesuit, this could happen. The next several national Dignity meetings—Miami in 1987, San Francisco in 1989, Washington in 1991, and New Orleans in 1993—all tried to exclude me from the speaker list, and only after the intervention of my friends was I allowed to speak.

New Orleans was, I felt, the final straw. After excluding me from the program, the committee in charge, I surmise, realized that the convention would be a failure unless they could lure more attendees, so at the last moment they invited me to speak. They issued a flyer which read "Come to New Orleans and hear John McNeill" in bold print and then listed the other speakers in smaller print. When I arrived in New Orleans, I discovered that I was obliged to pay for my own airfare and for my room at the hotel, and Charlie had to pay his own registration, whereas all the other speakers received a generous stipend, free registration for spouses or lovers, and free airfare and hotel rooms. When I complained, I was told that I was "old hat" and people were no longer interested in what I had to say, so I had been included only as a secondary speaker, an afterthought. I gave a talk on mature gay spirituality, which was well attended and well received. I was invited to speak once again to the national convention in Los Angeles in 1995 because of the special bond of our founding history I have with many of the members there.

One of my strongest supporters over the years has been Reverend Troy Perry, the founder of the Metropolitan Community Church, an all-inclusive church which welcomes gays, lesbians, transsexuals, and transgendered people. Troy invited me to dinner on my first visit to Los Angeles when I was on the book tour with *The Church and the Homosexual* in 1976. We have developed a close bond of friendship over the years because of his courageous and effective work for the gay and lesbian community and his continuous support of my ministry. I have frequently been invited to preach and give retreats and workshops at various Metropolitan Community Churches around the country. I was always grateful for the opportunities to preach the Word of God, denied to me in the Catholic church. I have always found the MCC communities to be warm, welcoming, and compassionate people, who take seriously the words of Isaiah: "My house shall be called a house of prayer for all peoples" (56:7).

The same summer as the Dignity convention in New Orleans, 1993, I had been invited to speak and give a workshop at the international convention of the Metropolitan Community Church in Phoenix. The MCC honored me with a special award for "bringing the message of the gospel to gay and lesbian people everywhere." I received such wonderful treatment, in total contrast to Dignity, that I made the decision to request of Troy that I be accepted into ministry in MCC. Troy was delighted and brought my request to the board of elders of MCC, and they agreed to accept me. However, when my pain receded and I brought my decision into prayer and counsel, I realized that to change allegiance, especially at my age, then sixty-eight, would be a big mistake. My ministry was primarily to my Catholic brothers and sisters; if I changed churches, I would lose much of my effectiveness. My identity was clearly that of a Roman Catholic priest, and I could not change that. I felt regret that I may have embarrassed Troy. I continue to preach on occasion and give retreats for my MCC brothers and sisters. I think that MCC of New York under the pastorship of Pat Bumgardner is one of the most inclusive and loving communities anywhere.

My relationship with Dignity was restored to its original warmth when President Marianne Duddy and the members of the national board invited me to the Dignity national convention in Boston in July 1997 to receive their first Prophetic Service Award, "in recognition of over 25 years of extraordinary work on behalf of the Catholic Gay, Lesbian, Bisexual and Transgendered Community."

Dignity New York, the chapter I helped found, invited me back to be celebrant and homilist at its twenty-fifth anniversary liturgy on October 26, 1997.

I have great admiration for the balance Dignity preserves in maintaining its respect and faith in the Catholic church while at the same time courageously confronting the inadequacies of the church's dogmatic teaching and pastoral practice.

26

The Trilogy Is Complete

The final volume of my trilogy on gay spirituality, *Freedom, Glorious Freedom: The Spiritual Journey to the Fullness of Life for Gays, Lesbians, and Everybody Else*, was published in hard copy by Beacon Press in 1995 and in paperback in 1996. This book was also published in Italian in 1996 as *Libertà, Gloriosa Libertà: Un cammino di spiritualità e liberazione per omosessuali credenti*. This book, in many ways, was the culmination of my years of philosophical and theological studies and of my clinical work and study in psychotherapy. I was able to integrate the philosophical reflections on freedom that came from my work on the philosophy of action of Maurice Blondel with the theological work on the freedom that results from the indwelling of the Spirit of God. I also dealt with the psychological process of freeing ourselves from the destructive patterns of the unconscious.

When we gays and lesbians discover that we cannot follow the fallible teachings of our religious authorities without destroying ourselves, we are forced to search out what God is saying to us through our experience and take personal responsibility for the choices we make. The first part of the book deals with freedom of conscience and discernment of spirits. These ancient practices of the Christian church have a special urgency for lesbian and gay people, who need to free themselves from all the homophobic authorities and deal with God on a direct and personal basis. The second part deals with the liberating process of coming out of the closet, seen as a spirit-filled effort to achieve the glory of God by becoming fully alive as gay and lesbian people. The third part deals with twelve-step spirituality as a spiritual process of liberation from all addictions that enables people to experience the love of God in its fullness. I explore the dialectic between the masculine and feminine ver-

sions of twelve-step spirituality and how gay people can integrate these dimensions into a holistic understanding of the spiritual process. The fourth
part deals with the problems that gay and lesbian people have in becoming
aware of God's special love for them and the unique qualities present in a gay
person's love for God. In the epilogue, I attempt to express a philosophical vision, looking to both the past and the future of how gay liberation fits into
Spirit-directed evolution of human history and its role in the ongoing struggle for human liberation. I explore the special gift we gay people have from
God of being whole persons fully in touch with everything masculine and feminine in ourselves. This wholeness allows the gay person to bring a new model
of human love into the world, a love based on mutuality and equality and no
longer based on domination and control.

With the publication of *Freedom, Glorious Freedom*, I undertook my third
book tour. I traveled to fifteen different cities to give lectures, retreats, and
workshops and appear on TV shows and radio talk shows. Two events stand
out: the first was an hour's conversation on television in Boston with Harvard
theologian Harvey Cox; the second occurred in Philadelphia. The President's
Committee on Sexual Minorities at St. Joseph's University invited me to participate in a dialogue with Dr. John Haas on "The Bible and Homosexuality:
Two Viewpoints." The day before the discussion was to take place Dr. Haas, a
professor from St. Charles Borromeo Seminary, refused to take part and the
panel was canceled. The reason Dr. Haas gave was that he had just seen my
book, *Freedom, Glorious Freedom*, the night before in Giovanni's Room, a gay
bookstore. In that book, he learned that I admit being in a gay relationship;
therefore, he felt that I did not have the moral character he required of a debate opponent. My own reading of what happened is that Dr. Haas saw the
chapter in my book dealing with "The Gay Friendly Attitude of Jesus and the
Early Christian Community!" and was not prepared to deal with the material
in that chapter.

Just as we were about to leave for the West Coast for visits to Seattle, San
Francisco, and Los Angeles, Charlie's mother was hospitalized, and he flew to
Hamilton, Ontario, to be with her. After several days in the hospital, she
seemed to recover and was scheduled to be released the next day to return
home. Charlie flew to join me in Los Angeles (I had already completed the
Seattle and San Francisco parts of the book tour), where we had dinner with

several leaders in the gay community: Troy Perry, Malcolm Boyd, Mark Thompson, Pat Colley, and Bruce Vaughn. That night, Charlie learned that his mother, instead of being released, had died suddenly during the night. We flew immediately to Hamilton to be with the family and for the funeral. I was pleased to discover that his family had included me in the obituary as Charlie's "special friend." Charlie and his older sister, Rose, have a close, loving bond, and she has always been very accepting and supportive of our relationship. A special bond of love has grown between Rose and me over the years, too, and she, as well as her five daughters and her son, have accepted me and treated me as a valued member of the family.

The final stage in my publishing history came with the trilogy of my books issued with uniform cover in May 1996. Once again, the only reviews that appeared were in the gay press. The secular press found the books too religious to be worthy of review. The mainline Christian press found them too pro-gay to be worthy of their notice. The one publication from which I had hoped for a review was the *National Catholic Reporter*. They had refused to review my previous book, *Taking a Chance on God*. Finally, a short put-down review appeared in the Booknotes column. I suffered a couple of sleepless nights because of my disappointment. Later, in response to several letters to the editor decrying the frivolousness of the brief review, the author of the review said that it had been eviscerated before being published.

Finally, during my morning meditation, I turned over to God the task of making my book known and asked God to be my publicity agent. Later that morning, I had a call from my friend Mary Hunt, who told me that she had completed a retrospective on my twenty-five years of pastoral work and publications on gay liberation and that the *National Catholic Reporter* had agreed to publish it. Once again, God answered my prayers, thanks be to God. The article appeared in the May 12, 1996, issue.

John McNeill: The Long View Is Short

The publication of John J. McNeill's trilogy in uniform paperback volumes (May 1996, Beacon Press) provides the occasion for an appreciative reflection on his work. How the Roman Catholic Church has changed, how John has changed, how we have all changed in the twenty years he spent "making a way where there was no way." It is early to assess the full impact (which I predict will see him labeled the contemporary equivalent of a Doctor of the Church), but preliminary analysis points toward the pivotal role he has carved out for himself in a changing church.

In 1976, when McNeill's book *The Church and the Homosexual* rocked the ecclesial world, there were no gay priests, no lesbian nuns, no bisexual people, no transgendered folk. Of course there were, but few had John McNeill's courage to raise the taboo issues and challenge kyriarchy on its own turf. He did for Catholicism what Stonewall did for the world; he fought back against those who would discriminate. The book earned him the opprobrium of Rome, but it also put the rest of us in his debt as he pioneered a struggle that by all Christian values ought to be long over by now yet, sadly, is still in full swing.

By the time he published *Taking a Chance on God* in 1988 the landscape had changed decisively. Dignity, Conference for Catholic Lesbians, Communications Ministry Inc., and New Ways Ministry were in full swing. Many dioceses and religious orders had support groups for their lesbian and gay members. Now John McNeill was offering the shoe for the other foot: if religions were not welcoming to lesbian, gay, bisexual and transgendered people, why should we be open to their raison d'etre, as it were, God? Given the treatment he suffered at the hands of ecclesial authorities, John McNeill had more than a little credibility on the topic. If he could believe, maybe I could.

With *Freedom, Glorious Freedom* in 1995, the subtitle tells all: The Spiritual Journey to the Fullness of Life for Gays, Lesbians, and Everybody Else." Now the real estate has been socialized and we who, like John, are church, whether members of the Metropolitan Community Church which was set up for us, or in the woman-church movement where we are more than welcome, or in the myriad denominationally-linked groups that carry the struggle for inclusion and meaning into the mainstream of Christian life. Of course John did not accomplish this single-handedly. But so many people trace their own understanding of Catholicism and homosexuality to some dimension of his work that it is fair to say he inspired an important theological movement that is now felt throughout the world.

John's story is well known. He is a good Irish Catholic from upstate New York who was taken prisoner during World War II. The literal kindness of strangers—people who risked their necks feeding prisoners—propelled him to consider a vocation in the Society of Jesus. He spent the next forty years as a Jesuit, including a decade of Vatican-enforced silence and then expulsion from the order. He moved along the Jesuit trajectory: novice, student, teacher, priest. He became a psychotherapist, a profession he still practices in New York City, but retains a priestly, and even Jesuitic way about him.

In *Freedom, Glorious Freedom* he describes much of what happened to him along the way, especially how his spiritual life was enriched by being gay and *vice versa*. He does not strike out against those who wronged him, but describes with remarkable equanimity how the same Jesuit "discernment of spirits" brought him to coming out and speaking out. The steady support of his lover of three decades, Charles Chiarelli, shines through.

It is finally the cogency of his position on the need to live with coherence between truth and appearance that propelled John McNeill to a mature, healthy self-acceptance and an equally mature, healthy insistence that the rest of the church do the same. It is this message that he shares with clients and audiences, this congruency between what you see and what you get that makes him the envy of many a closeted clergyman. It makes a big difference.

I see three major changes in the rest of us that have accompanied John McNeill in these two decades. First, the question of homosexuality, far from being a taboo topic, is a central issue on the church's agenda. Whether one likes it or not, the closet doors of good Catholic homes, rectories and convents have swung open with style. Few are the Catholic families who do not number at least one "out" person among their extended kin. Virtually all religious orders and dioceses are coping with the results of such truth-telling, and finding that life goes on as it did before, when they relax and discover the truth about some of their best and brightest. This requires some readjustment of categories and assumptions, but it results in mature and healthy communities, made up of mature and healthy people.

We who are "out" vacillate between being condemned by some and acting as role models for others. I can only imagine what John McNeill must have felt in those early days when he was instrumental in getting Dignity off the ground and when he was being assailed from all sides by those who opposed his very being. Now he is viewed as a wise man, an elder who is respected by his community, a community made up mostly of gay men, with many appreciative lesbian and heterosexual friends as well. I have watched these gay men flock to John, not in a cheap search for the fathers they didn't have, but in honest admiration for the man he is, and in search of the men they'd like to become. Role models don't come cheap.

A second major change is the increase in honesty he has encouraged. I did not have the privilege of knowing him then, though I was a child in Syracuse during his LeMoyne College teaching years. It is said that one can take a man out of the Jesuits but not the Jesuit out of the man. This is true. But what John has become is an honest man in love, in sharp contrast to so many of his confreres who love with fear, or who just fear. He does not need to hide Charlie under a bushel basket, pretend that he is celibate, nor choose between ministry and marriage. He has it all, and de facto makes clear that others who are lucky in love can be equally honest and successful, indeed we ought to be, as I like to think of it, "for the greater glory of God."

I suspect that this must rankle some of his colleagues, especially the gay ones (whom I would guess are the majority of the community that ousted him, another painful piece of this chapter in church history). John's seeming sacrifice years ago—first accepting silencing, then paying the price for speaking out— has resulted in his living to enjoy the fruits of his labor as a gay priest. In fact the Irish in him comes forth when he says with a twinkle in his eye that his tombstone will read "Here Lies a Gay Priest Who Took a Chance on God!" He plans to be buried (no time soon, please God) at Kirkridge, an ecumenical conference center in Pennsylvania that has for two decades with his leadership been a welcoming home to thousands of lesbian, gay, bisexual and transgendered Christians who have been battered by their churches.

A third change because of John McNeill's work is the foundation we now have for an inclusive Catholic theology. McNeill's early scholarly work was based on the thought of Maurice Blondel, who was a forerunner of sorts of the contemporary liberation theologians, a philosopher who insisted on actions speaking louder than words. John is never far from the fray, but neither is he far from the contemplative life that gives birth to much of his writing. He is as at home as the grand marshal of a gay pride parade as he is celebrating mass, as much himself quoting Aquinas as John Boswell, as much at work praying as counseling, as much enraged by racism as homo hatred. He preaches and offers retreats, lectures and inspires audiences around the country—even in Rome when invited—with an enthusiasm and openness that are contagious. Cynics among us probably would have given up on God, Jesus, the Church, the Jesuits, long ago had we experienced John McNeill's trials. But he keeps building on the foundation he built, a master craftsman in the guild of love.

The trilogy is now complete, though I figure John McNeill for at least another book, maybe more. People who pick up the first volume today are reading church history. The second volume is a kind of prolegomenon to the lesbian/gay theology now taking shape. The third is a treatise on spirituality equal to so many important works in the field. Those with eyes to see will soon realize that there is a treasure in their library, just as we have a treasure in our midst.

The fact that this retrospective came from the pen of Mary Hunt was an unexpected and delightful surprise for me. Mary and her lover, Diann Neu, have been friends of ours for many years. Mary is a brilliant theologian and a forceful and insightful proponent of feminist theology and spirituality. She is a founder of Woman's Alliance for Theology, Ethics and Ritual (WATER), a powerful proponent of women's contribution and rights in the church. Mary and Diann have worked together for many years trying to organize women in South and Central America.

Mary and I have served together on several occasions as presenters at the annual Lesbian and Gay Christian retreat at Kirkridge. I have not always agreed with Mary, but she always came up with insights that made me reconsider my position. On one occasion dealing with death and immortality, Mary argued that the need for personal immortality is strictly a male need. Women are content to "sink back into the creative matrix out of which new life comes." I strongly disagreed with Mary, arguing that the need for personal immortality was a universal human need totally independent of male or female issues. I named Mary's theory "the compost pile theory of immortality."

Mary, among other feminist theologians, made me aware that we are in a special moment of universal spiritual liberation in terms of women's liberation. This, like gay liberation, is I believe, the work of the Holy Spirit in our day. All of us are challenged to come into contact with the feminine not just outside ourselves but also within ourselves. This is the primary process I have been involved with in the case of many of the gay male clients who have come to me for therapy. At the heart of most cases of internalized male homophobia lies an even deeper and more intensely repressed *feminaphobia*. Many of my gay clients had thoroughly repressed the feminine and are afraid of it.

Many in their earlier years were very open to and in touch with the feminine self. However, because of the homophobia of their family, church, and culture, they had to learn to try to control and repress any evidence of that feminine self. This meant trying to repress all feelings, all creativity and all spirituality, and also trying to live "in their heads" by developing their intellectual skills and compulsively staying out of touch with all feelings. The only way to health and fullness of life for these clients is to unrepress and live out that previously dreaded feminine dimension of themselves. I believe that the dialogue going on at present between feminist and traditional understandings of spirituality gives us a unique opportunity to understand the principal challenges that feminists are bringing to help all of us grow to complete maturity. In my own therapy, it was by undoing my own feminaphobia that I was able to make progress toward mature mental health as a gay man.

In the epilogue of *Freedom, Glorious Freedom*, I argued that the hope of humanity for a happier and fuller life would be the emergence of a visible group that can live out fully its masculine and feminine dimensions without the need to repress either. We need a group who will model the ideal goal of humanity's present evolution, people who can keep their masculine and feminine dimensions in good equilibrium and bring forth a balanced synthesis of the two. This, I believe, is the providential role of the gay and lesbian political and spiritual groups that have come into being over the past twenty-five years. Every dialectical movement toward a higher synthesis, if it is to succeed, must carry the seed of its resolution within itself. I believe that both of us, gay men and lesbian women, have a role to play in human history, a role that would be seriously jeopardized if we should continue to conform to an "either-or" understanding of masculine and feminine development.

The gay spiritual movement has emerged out of the heart of the world to play a decisive role in bringing about this synthesis. The only way, however, that gays and lesbians can play this role is to overcome their fears and have the courage to come out of the closet. They must model in a very public way their ability to balance the masculine and feminine dimensions within themselves, their ability to put together genuine gay human love for each other with a deep spiritual life, and their awareness of the presence of the Holy Spirit in their lives.

27

Sister Sheila

One of the greatest blessings in my life, a blessing for which I am profoundly grateful, is my sister, Sister Sheila. After many years of illness, Sis died on November 17, 1996. She was one of the people I loved most deeply. All my life my sister played a special role. After my mother died when I was four, Sis, who was two years older than I, took over and mothered me. Sis often put both our geography books in her bookbag so that, if anyone bothered us on our way to and from school, she could let them have it. Whenever I got a bad report card and was afraid of incurring Katie's wrath, Sis faked Katie's signature on the report card. She was the perfect big sister.

Sis loved me deeply and prayed for me all my life. Ron Sams, a fellow Jesuit, told me that when he was serving mass at a parish church where Sis was the sacristan during World War II, she asked him to pray for her brother, who was "missing in action." Not until we were ordained together at Fordham many years later did he realize that I was that brother. It was Ron whom Sis chose to be homilist at her funeral.

Sis once told me that she was offering up all her prayers and sufferings that I might persevere in the priesthood. Consequently, my greatest fear, when I was expelled from the Jesuits, was that Sis would feel that all her prayers had been unheard. But Sis never lost faith in me. She completely supported me in my ministry to gays and lesbians. She once told me that a member of her community who ran a hospital in Africa came to her while home in Buffalo on vacation to tell her how much my book *The Church and the Homosexual* meant to her. Most of her hospital staff were gay men. After reading my book, she felt comfortable and was able to work with them. She asked Sis to thank me.

At the Jesuit retreat house in Guelph, Ontario, a fellow retreatant introduced herself to Sis and told her that she was an Episcopal priest. My books had been a very real help to her in dealing with her lesbian and gay congregants. She asked Sis to convey her gratitude to me. These incidents and many others gave Sis confidence that my work was in conformity with the Spirit of God.

Sis had a beautiful rainbow stole made for me and asked me to wear it whenever I preached to gay groups. That stole adorned her casket at her funeral. Whenever I was giving a retreat, Sis enlisted the prayers of her community and the various charismatic prayer groups to which she belonged on behalf of my ministry to my gay brothers and lesbian sisters. While in the infirmary of the mother house, Saint Mary of the Angels, in Williamsville, New York, she enlisted the prayers of the other elderly nuns there. Having so many elderly nuns praying for your ministry is truly extraordinary prayer power. I frequently felt the powerful presence of the Holy Spirit in the room during my retreats, and I attributed that to Sis and her companions' prayers.

My sister suffered an incredible amount of physical pain and discomfort over the past forty years. Because of a condition of bone deterioration, her mobility was continually reduced over the years. She underwent innumerable operations, frequently with complications. She once shared with me a passage from a book of spirituality she had included in her diary that meant a great deal to her:

> Once we know that suffering has a purpose, or at least we can believe that there is a meaning to it, we can endure much worse. That is the Gospel message—that suffering need not be a loss. People can grow better through suffering, and can also become beautiful, and the latter serve as a grace to others. Their suffering has made them transparent, more open, wise and gentle; in them we see the fruitfulness of the cross. Pain can glorify us, make us radiant and give a fruitfulness to our lives.

Pain had certainly given my sister an enviable spiritual power and freedom. Ten years ago, she told me about something that happened while she was on her annual retreat at the Jesuit retreat house in Guelph. On the first day of the retreat, she found herself in a profound depression that felt like death itself. Sis normally experienced peace and seldom was depressed. This depression lasted all day, and no matter how she tried she could not lift it. Exhausted after a day spent in depressed suffering, she returned to her room and began to write in her diary the events, thoughts, and feelings of that day. Suddenly she began to write rapidly, and she felt that someone else was guiding her hand. These were the words she read after the automatic writing came to an end:

> Sheila, don't be afraid of death. I have freed you of many things, so that you can prayerfully prepare for my kingdom. Have no fear because your goodness and love for me have far outweighed your faults and mistakes.
>
> Continue to love me with your great love and the generosity of your life that you have given to me. You are beautiful to me. I love you with a deep love because you have accepted my will. I will continue to love and bless you. Do not be afraid. I will be with you always to give you courage and the strength you need.

From that moment, Sis told me, the depression lifted, and she has known a wonderful joy and lightness of heart and felt ready for anything that might come along. Her best friend told me that, at the time of Sis's death, Sis understood that her experience of automatic writing was her share in the transfiguration and that God made clear to her that God would ask her to share in the agony in the garden. God was asking her to accept a share in the sufferings of Christ for the salvation of the world.

Sis enjoyed life; she loved people, especially children. She also enjoyed going out on occasion to a good restaurant with her friends. Certainly, for the next ten years, Sis's suffering intensified. She developed throat cancer and underwent constant treatment, chemotherapy, radiation, and laser therapy, to no avail. Eventually, Sis's cancer metastasized and became a bone cancer that spread throughout her body. After innumerable trips to Roswell Hospital in Buffalo in the last months of her life, Sis had to leave her convent for a hospice, where she felt in exile. In the last week of her life, she was able to return to the convent, and her fellow religious kept her company day and night until the end. Her cancer at the end was breaking all the bones in her body. She was in terrible pain and had to be heavily sedated. Just a few days before her death, I was able to visit her, and for the first time she admitted that the pain had become more than she could bear and she was asking God to take her. I prayed for God to let me take some of that pain so that Sis could die in peace.

Sis died peacefully at 3 A.M. on November 17, 1996. I was speaking that day at Call to Action in Detroit, and all my listeners joined me in a special prayer for Sis. In *Our Greatest Gift* (San Francisco: Harper, 1994), Henri Nouwen made the point that every baptized person has the power to make their greatest gift after death; they have the power to send out the Holy Spirit on the world and all those they love. So I expect that Sis's love and prayers will be with me in the future as I continue my ministry. I am certain that the success I have known in my ministry of bringing the message of God's acceptance and love for gays and lesbians was as much, if not more, due to Sis's suffering and prayers as to any talents or skills that God has given to me. We formed a great spiritual team together. During the last three years of her life, Sis prayed a novena for the sale of my house without avail. But one month after her death, our house was sold in the middle of winter after being three years on the market. I attribute the miracle of that sale to Sis's influence.

Shortly after my sister's death, I had one of the most moving dreams of my whole life concerning Katie. I attribute the dream to Sis's spirit of reconciliation. In the dream, I returned to Katie's house, which I had not visited for many years. The house seemed deserted, but suddenly I heard a noise upstairs and knew it was Katie. I started up the stairway, calling out to her. Suddenly I saw her at the head of the stairs. She cried out in joy when she saw me. She ran to me sobbing, and we heartily embraced. Somehow or other, I felt that a profound reconciliation took place between us. I awakened full of joy and gratitude.

One other relative who has stayed in contact with me and supported my gay ministry is my nephew, Timothy McNeill. Tim is my deceased brother Tom's only son. I have a fond memory of teaching him as a child to tie his own shoelaces. After graduating from Canisius High School and the University of Buffalo, Tim traveled overseas and stayed in a monastery in Nepal, where he became a Buddhist. He spent several years in the Himalayan region, including three years as a volunteer in the Peace Corps in Afghanistan.

We made contact again when he came to New York City from Afghanistan to continue his education at Columbia University. After his many years of Buddhist meditation, I observed that he had an ethereal quality of peace and detachment. It was then that he revealed to me that he was gay.

Tim moved on to Boston to attend the Kennedy School of Government at Harvard. After several years of working for the development of Third World countries, Tim was asked by his Tibetan lama to take over as publisher of Wisdom Publications, which brings the Buddhist message to the English-speaking world. Tim has not only encouraged and supported me in my gay ministry but also introduced me to the spiritual riches of Buddhist meditation. At present he lives in Cambridge, Massachusetts, with his lover, Jim.

28

The Saging

Another highlight of my ministry occurred at the June 1994 retreat for gay men at Kirkridge. The retreatants organized a special ritual, "The Saging of John McNeill: A ritual honoring the leadership of John McNeill and our gay elders, and celebrating the wisdom of the gay male community" prepared and led by Ken White and John Linscheid and carried out by the gay men in attendance at Kirkridge. This was the text of the ritual:

We need to continue to find appropriate ways (like ritual) to reflect our experiences, rediscover and pass on our history, remember those who have gone on before, and tell stories about the importance and worth of gay men in history and contemporary society. We need to do this in meaningful and powerful ways within our community. We, as individual gay men, and as community, have a deep spiritual need to find ways to welcome gay men into the community and pass along the wisdom, the learning about life passages, the secrets of survival and celebration of gay culture. Historically rituals were the way the tribes and communities formally communicated important group knowledge to their members. Rites of passage are those structures, rituals, and ceremonies by which members and individuals in a group successfully come to know who they are and what they are about. Through rites of passage, they find the purpose and the meaning of their existence, as they proceed from one clearly defined state of existence to the next stage or passage in their life.

John has a significant family here at Kirkridge. The family gathers every year, adding siblings as we go. In our gatherings, John has taught us valuable lessons of gay experience. I particularly hold fast his insight that "good theology results in good psychology and vice versa." Religion that destroys physical or mental health is pathological and does not contribute to the glory of God. For me personally, at a time when I was facing my father's death, John passed on the wisdom of learning to embrace death as a friend and transition into the arms of

God. So John was already fulfilling his role as an elder in the gay community in the years before we recognized him as a Sage.

Our saging of John McNeill was simply a recognition of the contribution John has made over the years to our gay community. He has functioned as a priest and elder among us and it seemed to be time to hold him up. As we deal with issues of gay aging, we felt that there was no better way to focus our ritual than through the recognition of John as a Sage among us.

At the end, the community presented me with a purple stole and a six-foot staff made of polished mahogany and proclaimed me "Elder." I felt healed in a very special way from the deep wounds in my psyche that resulted from expulsion from my Jesuit community. To me, the ceremony was the equivalent of being made a bishop by acclamation in the context of the Kirkridge gay and lesbian community.

29

Toward Spiritual Maturity

If I can abstract one lesson from my spiritual journey that transcends my own personal spiritual growth and has, I believe, a universal application in today's church, it is the lesson on spiritual maturity. I formulated that lesson in this talk I gave to Call to Action at their 1996 session in Detroit.

Mature Spirituality: The Holy Spirit, Founder of a Democratic Church

My topic today, Mature Spirituality, is the fruit of my twenty-six years of ministry to my lesbian sisters and gay brothers. My initial years of work in gay ministry as a priest and psychotherapist made me keenly aware of the enormous amount of pain, psychological trauma, and potential emotional breakdown present in many Christian gays and lesbians. I became aware that most gay people who came to me for counseling had interiorized church teaching on homosexuality. The result was deep psychic woundedness, self-hatred, and the tendency to base their relationship with God on fear. Most gays see themselves created with their orientation by God. To tell them, as the Vatican has, that their orientation is an "orientation to evil," they hear it as saying that God created them with their desire to reach out in love as a profound evil. We read in scripture: God is love, and if anyone loves they know God. But the church's message is: If you gays reach out in love to each other, you are guilty of serious sins. This would mean that God is sadistic. Such a god can be related to only out of fear and, if perfect love casts out fear, it is equally true that perfect fear casts out all love. So, it quickly became apparent to me that what was destructive psychologically had to be bad theology. If gays and lesbians are to have healthy and holy lives, they have to break off their dependence on the extrinsic authority of the church and develop a mature spirituality.

I entered into psychotherapy to deal with my own psychic traumas, and I dedicated my personal spiritual life to the task of developing that mature spirituality. In my last two books, *Taking a Chance on God: Liberating Theology for Gays, Lesbians, and Their Lovers, Families, and Friends* (1988) and *Freedom, Glo-*

rious Freedom: The Spiritual Journey to the Fullness of Life for Gays, Lesbians, and Everybody Else (1995), I attempted to spell out what that psychological and spiritual maturity meant and how to go about that growth in maturity both psychologically and spiritually.

Every one of us is characterized by a ravenous spiritual hunger. Sometimes this hunger is a consciously felt need—more often it is a hidden one—experienced simply as depression, numbness, and the feeling that life is meaningless. How can we develop a mature spiritual life that speaks to our profound needs, especially those of us who are estranged from the institutional church?

A healthy maturing process is one by which we separate off from dependence on external authorities, become autonomous adults, make our own choices, and take responsibility for those choices. On both the psychological and spiritual levels, maturity is the ability to discern what is the true self and to find the courage to act out that true self, the ability to live our lives according to our own insights and feelings, no longer attempting to live our lives in a continuous effort to meet the expectations of others.

St. Bernard of Clairvaux once made the observation: "Spiritual life is like living water that springs up from the very depth of our own spiritual experience. In spiritual life everyone has to drink from his or her own well." The first mark, then, of a healthy adult spiritual life is that it will be based on personal experience.

At the Last Supper, Jesus pointed out the maturing process that his disciples would have to go through. At one point he said to them: "It is necessary that I should go away in order for the Spirit to come" (summary of John 16:6–13). Jesus was pointing out that his disciples must detach themselves from their dependence on his extrinsic presence and prepare themselves to receive the Spirit of God, who will dwell in their hearts.

A central Christian teaching attributed to Jesus himself is without doubt of utmost importance for Christian spiritual maturity, and that is *freedom of conscience*. Vatican II spelled out that teaching in this statement from the Pastoral Constitution of the Church in the Modern World: "Humans have in their heart a law written by God. To obey it is the dignity of the human; according to it we will be judged. There we are alone with God, whose voice echoes in our depths."

This teaching is based on Jesus' promise to his followers to send them the Holy Spirit, who will dwell in their hearts. At the Last Supper, Jesus promised: "I will ask the Father, and he will give you another Advocate, to be with you forever. This is the Spirit of truth, whom the world cannot receive" (John 14:16–17). Jesus further declared: "I have said these things to you while I am still with you. But the Advocate, the Holy Spirit, whom the Father will send in my name, will teach you everything, and remind you of all that I have said to you" (John 14:25–26).

The author of the epistle to the Hebrews sees the gift of the Holy Spirit as a fulfillment of this prophecy of Jeremiah: "The days are surely coming, says the LORD, when I will make a new covenant with the house of Israel and the house of Judah. It will not be like the covenant that I made with their ancestors when I took them by the hand to bring them out of the land of Egypt —a covenant that they broke, though I was their husband, says the LORD. But this is the covenant that I will make with the house of Israel after those days, says the LORD: I will put my law within them, and I will write it on their hearts; and I will be their God, and they shall be my people. No longer shall they teach one another, or say to each other, 'Know the LORD,' for they shall all know me, from the least of them to the greatest, says the LORD; for I will forgive their iniquity, and remember their sin no more" (Jeremiah 31:31–34).

Notice that Jeremiah foresees the new covenant, where every human being from the least to the greatest will have direct access to a God who dwells in their heart. This access to God will not be the privilege of a few who are gifted with extraordinary intelligence, or ritual rank, or even special holiness. The Holy Spirit is a thoroughgoing respecter of democratic process. There is no hint here that one must go to authorities in order to inform one's conscience; God directly and immediately informs our consciences, including those of lesbians and gays.

In the Acts of the Apostles on Pentecost Sunday, Peter recalls these words of the prophet Joel: "In the last days it will be, God declares, that I will pour out my Spirit upon all flesh, and your sons and your daughters shall prophesy, and your young men shall see visions, and your old men shall dream dreams. Even upon my slaves, both men and women, in those days I will pour out my Spirit; and they shall prophesy" (Acts 2:17–18). Once again, the emphasis is placed on the democratic nature of the Spirit.

At the Last Supper, Jesus informed his disciples that it was necessary that he should go away in order for the Spirit to come. "But because I have said these things to you, sorrow has filled your hearts. Nevertheless I tell you the truth: it is to your advantage that I go away, for if I do not go away, the Advocate will not come to you; but if I go, I will send him to you. . . . When the Spirit of truth comes, he will guide you into all the truth" (John 16:6–7, 13a).

Why could the Spirit come only after Jesus' death? Because as long as Jesus remained alive and present, his disciples had their center of authority outside themselves and were not, therefore, fully mature and totally responsible for their actions. They were striving to meet the expectations of someone else. They had not yet become fully creative and responsible adults. But after Jesus' death, his Spirit became what Paul saw as the source of the glorious freedom of the children of God: "And because you are children, God has sent the Spirit of his Son into our hearts, crying, 'Abba! Father!' So you are no longer a slave but a child, and if a child then also an heir, through God" (Galatians 4:6–7). The Greek word *ecclesia* originally indicated a gathering of equals with no superior or inferior.

Paul clearly understood the good news of the *evangelium*, the gospel message, is exactly the message of our freedom: "For freedom Christ has set us free. Stand firm, therefore, and do not submit again to a yoke of slavery" (Galatians 5:1). Christians are free because their God is a God of love who has adopted them into his family: "For all who are led by the Spirit of God are children of God. For you did not receive a spirit of slavery to fall back into fear, but you have received a spirit of adoption. When we cry, 'Abba! Father!' it is that very Spirit bearing witness with our spirit that we are children of God, and if children, then heirs, heirs of God and joint heirs with Christ" (Romans 8:14–17a).

Paul continually repeats the theme that God's Spirit dwells within us and, if we ask, will empower us: "Likewise the Spirit helps us in our weakness; for we do not know how to pray as we ought, but that very Spirit intercedes with sighs too deep for words" (Romans 8:26).

There is a yearning and a longing deep in our psyche which is not just that of our ego but that of the Spirit of God dwelling in the depths of our spirit. Maurice Blondel gives a philosophical expression to this same theme in his philosophy of action: "Our God dwells within us, and the only way to become one with our God is to become one with our authentic self." To be *authentic* means that we are in touch with the true self, that our spirit and the Spirit of God dwelling within us are in harmony.

With the death of Jesus, then, and the coming of the Spirit, the apostles received a challenge as well as an opportunity to mature. As Paul expressed it, "until all of us come to the unity of the faith and of the knowledge of the Son of God, to maturity, to the measure of the full stature of Christ" (Ephesians 4:13). They had to give up the security of a provident leader; they had to find out what God wanted from them from within themselves and their own experience. It was only after the coming of the Holy Spirit that the apostles found the courage to leave the security of their closet (the upper room) and go out into the world as responsible adult agents of the Spirit.

In like manner in our spiritual life, we must pass from a passive, dependent role to an active, creative one. We have a special need to become mature, self-motivated, autonomous people, no longer passively dependent on outside sources for a sense of our identity and well-being. We must not let our enemies outside ourselves define us; we must let the Spirit of love that dwells within our hearts define us. If we approach church authorities, it should not be to get an approval that they cannot and will not give us. Rather, it should be to bear witness to what the Holy Spirit is saying to us through our experience.

Liberation from oppression is a true value of the gospel. However, we must become aware that Christian freedom comes from within through the Spirit of Christ, and we must realize that that freedom is something to be claimed, not something that is granted by external authority. We must listen to the Spirit within us, listen to the voice of the oppressed around us, and then act for human rights and equality.

It is this understanding of the role of the Holy Spirit that gives me great consolation during these times when the church reacts to its gay members in ignorance and even downright hostility. We should all be grateful to God for creating a humanly fallible church. We are intensely aware that, if our parents had been infallible, we could never have grown up and matured to become autonomous and responsible adults. We would spend our lives saying, "Yes, Mother," "Yes, Father." We would never be able to develop our own capacity for independent judgment and, consequently, never feel personally responsible for our actions. God blessed us with finite and fallible parents. It was precisely when our parents proved fallible that we were challenged to take distance from their authority, then make our own choices, and be fully responsible.

In a similar way, we are dependent on the fallibility of religious authorities in order to develop an adult freedom of conscience. When, for example, we gays and lesbians discover that we cannot follow the fallible teachings of our religious authorities without destroying ourselves, then we are forced to search out what God is saying to us through our experience and take personal responsibility for the choices we make. I believe that the Holy Spirit is using the fallibility of our religious authorities to guide the entire Christian community into a new level of maturity and responsibility necessary for the spiritual growth of the human community in today's world. We can no longer afford to be "Eichmann Christians," claiming that our only responsibility is to be obedient to authorities but we have no personal responsibility for the consequences of our actions.

There are two ways to relate to the church that are both immature, that is, to be in the church as an *uncritical lover* or as an *unloving critic*. Either of these paths leads to the destruction of the church. And there are two mature ways to belong to the democratic church of the Spirit, as a *critical lover* or a *loving critic*. The primary responsibility of members of the democratic church of the Spirit is to become people of deep prayer, seeking constantly to hear what the Spirit says to them through their experience. The primary responsibility of authority in the church of the Spirit is to listen to what the Spirit is saying to them through the experience of the people of God.

In the document "The Church in the Modern World of Vatican II," lay people are urged to accept their responsibility to apply Christian principles in the area of their expertise: "Laymen should also know that it is generally the function of their well-formed Christian conscience to see that the divine law is inscribed in the life of the earthly city. From priests they may look for spiritual light and nourishment. Let the lay person not imagine, however, that his pastors are always such experts that to every problem which arises, however complicated, they can readily give him a concrete solution or that such is their mission. Rather, enlightened by Christian wisdom and giving close attention to the teaching authority of the Church, let the layman take on his own distinctive role."

This was the experience of the American bishops when they prepared to write their encyclicals on the economy and nuclear warfare by holding hearings with all the parties concerned and listening carefully to what the Spirit was saying to them through the people of God. When the bishops began the process of writing an encyclical on the role of women in the church, they began again by listening carefully to groups of women from all segments of the church. Rome intervened, saying the bishops misunderstood. It was their task to *teach* and not to *listen*. Rome then tried to dictate the content of the encyclical, with the result that the bishops realized that such a statement would only make matters worse and ceased trying to write the encyclical.

Every time the present church tries to exercise what is popularly referred to as "creeping infallibility," it tends to issue authoritative statements that are out of touch with the experience of the people of God. This is especially true in the area of sexual ethics. The hierarchy seems more concerned with preserving the authority of the institution than with promoting the true happiness and well-being, both psychological and spiritual, of the faithful. The result is that the faithful, following the guidance of the Spirit within, are "nonreceptive" of authoritarian teaching.

We must then "learn to drink from our own wells." We must learn to place our trust in our own direct experience of life and what those experiences reveal to us. We must trust that God speaks immediately and directly through our own experiences and that these experiences are the only "unpolluted waters" from which we can drink. In the process of drinking from the well of our own experiences, we must try to relearn step by step to trust God and to trust what God is saying to us directly. This is the ancient Christian doctrine of "discernment of spirits."

The way to know God and to become intimate with God is to listen carefully to what your own feelings are telling you. God speaks to us primarily, not through our intellect but through our hearts—that is, through our emotions—and it is by listening with our hearts that we can hear what God is saying to us.

The theologians of the Middle Ages had a saying: "You can grasp God with your mind, *never*. You can grasp God with your heart, *ever*." If your experience brings with it feelings of deep peace, quiet, and joy, then you know that the message coming through your heart is God saying, "Right on! You are one with the Spirit of God and there is growth in intimacy between us." However, if you perform an action that contradicts the Spirit of God dwelling in your heart, then you will know turmoil, depression, and sadness.

Václav Havel believes that the development of a free conscience will be essential for the development of competent political and religious leaders in the future. These are the words he spoke to a joint session of the United States Congress: "Souls, individual spirituality, firsthand personal insight into things, the courage to be yourself and go the way your conscience points; humility in the face of the mysterious order of being, confidence in its natural direction, and, above all, trust in your own subjectivity as your principal link with the subjectivity of the world—these are the qualities the politicians of the future must cultivate."

I would like to end with a special prayer to the Holy Spirit for a new Pentecost for the church we love, that all of us, authorities and faithful alike, may with God's grace be fully open to the message the Spirit is speaking in our hearts and be open to what the Spirit is saying through all the people of God and, especially, the outcasts.

Come, Holy Spirit, and fill all our hearts with the Spirit of divine love.

30

My Spiritual Life Today

I am now seventy-three years old. I have discovered that every decade of my life has been happier and more peaceful than the last. Each decade has brought with it greater intimacy with a God of mercy and love and a greater trust in God's love for me. As my body grows older, my spirit becomes younger. I know this is a gift from God for which I am grateful. As the years have gone by, my prayer life has undergone a radical change, from a prayer of the head, a prayer of words, concepts, and thought processes, to a prayer of the heart. God has given me the grace to be continuously aware of a longing in my heart for a greater intimacy with God. My awareness of God is based on what I am deprived of, what I need and don't have, what I am yearning for, what I have a hunger and thirst for and have not yet achieved.

Privation is a paradoxical concept. Philosophers define *privation* as "the absence of that which ought to be." Privation, then, is an experience of absence in presence or presence in absence. To experience God as privation, then, necessarily means that I have already had an experience of God's presence. I like to compare it to a missing piece in a jigsaw puzzle. If I see it, I will know it because there is only one piece that will fit into that empty space. In St. Augustine's words, "You made us for Yourself, O Lord, and our hearts will never rest until they rest in You."

My personal knowledge of God has little to do with any intellectual definition. All the great mystics saw our efforts to capture God with thoughts and concepts as self-defeating. They recommended in prayer that we should empty our minds of thoughts and concepts and enter the "cloud of unknowing."

My knowledge of God, then, comes from the hunger and thirst in myself. In the words of Psalm 63:1:

> O God, you are my God, I seek you,
>   my soul thirsts for you;
> my flesh faints for you,
>   as in a dry and weary land
>   where there is no water.

My prayer life consists of being in touch with that hunger and thirst, not letting anything fill it in or block it off, or hide it from me. Rather, I strive to be in touch with that hunger and thirst, to consecrate it by converting it intentionally into prayer and identifying with it. My prayer life, then, is very simple. I spend a lot of time just being in touch with that longing, being open to it, and waiting. I continually ask God to come and meet that deep deprivation within me. I am like a desert waiting for the rain to come and soak in. As a result, my prayer is continuous.

I set aside time to enter into myself, empty out all thoughts and rest in the presence of God, and experience the longing for that presence. I also spend some time every day "praying" the *New York Times*, formulating a prayer appropriate to every headline and article. In this way, I strive to let my prayer reach out to the whole world.

At a recent Easter vigil, the liturgy at sundown on the Saturday before Easter Sunday, I heard this passage from the Psalms: "As a deer longs for flowing streams, so my soul longs for you, O God" (42:1). Suddenly, I was in touch with a profound longing for union with God, a longing that was at the same time painful and pleasurable, and I began to cry. I am grateful to God for that moment and see it as a great grace. Since that time, I am consciously aware that what I want is intimacy with God, and I will not settle for anything less. I am aware that being in touch with that longing is already a kind of awareness of God through privation. This awareness is God's gift and promise. All other touches of intimacy in my life—intimacies of family, friendships, and my intimacy with my lover, Charlie—are foretastes of that ultimate intimacy. But the only intimacy that can meet my needs and fill my heart is the intimacy with God. I particularly love the words of St. Augustine's prayer in his *Confessions*:

> Late have I loved you, O Beauty, ever ancient, ever new; late have I loved you!
> You were within me, but I was outside, and it was there that I searched for you.
> In my unloveliness I plunged into the lovely things which you created.

You were with me, but I was not with you. Created things kept me from you; yet if they had not been in you they would not have been at all.

You called, you shouted, and you broke through my deafness. You flashed, you shone, and you dispelled my blindness. You breathed your fragrance on me; I drew in breath and now I pant for you. I have tasted you, now I hunger and thirst for more. You touched me, and now I long for your peace.

The great spiritual leaders of the past have always taught that God in fact nurtures our growth in capacity and potential for a passionate intimate relationship with God. My own experience of spiritual development finds its closest description in the understanding of spiritual growth in the writings of Gregory of Nyssa. Gregory describes beautifully the step-by-step nature of spiritual growth. He says that God always waits on our freedom. Our first serious *yes!* to God enables divine love to begin to act within us. Our inner space—as a result of that *yes!*—is then ready to receive something of God. God fills that space as fully as we are able to accept. At the same time, this filling enlarges the space, and we long for more. Thus, the lover of God is always filled to his or her capacity and always longs for more of God. Yet the longing does not bring frustration because there is a fullness. According to St. Gregory, this process goes on beyond death into eternity because God is infinite and we are always a finite capacity open to further growth in our identity with an infinite God. For all eternity, we continue to grow deeper and deeper in union with a God who is infinite and, therefore, can never be exhausted.

The most difficult spiritual struggle for me is the endeavor to center myself in God and the love of God versus the ravenous hunger in my ego to make itself the center of my universe. I am aware of a very real danger: that if God gives me even a taste of the joy of God's presence and love, my ego could go completely out of control. I am likely to start searching to experience God's love as an ego fix, trying to use God as an object for my own ego satisfaction and my own feelings of superiority and specialness. Of course, God will not let God's self be used in this way. In God's goodness, God allows my spirit to be plunged into a "dark night of the soul," until I am ready to experience God's love in such a way that it only contributes to the "greater glory of God!"

I understand well the Sufi prayer: "Give me the pain of your love, O Lord, and not the joy. Give the joy to others, but give me the pain!" The pain of God's love is the longing for that love from a sense of deprivation. That pain purifies me and makes me ready to experience the positive joy of God's presence. So in moments of dark night, I make an act of trust that through this emptiness and privation God is purifying me and making me ready to share in God's joy.

How do I go about lessening the grip of my ego on my spiritual life? The word *ego* has very different meanings in psychotherapy and in spirituality. In psychotherapy, the *ego* refers to the ability of the I or the self to transpose the chaos of raw experience, id drives, and the like onto a meaningful and conscious plane. Building the psychological ego implies promoting one's consciousness, fostering ego development, channeling energy from the id and the superego into the ego, and taking responsibility for one's self and one's unconscious. To explain this in spiritual terms, I can be cocreator of my very being in cooperation with the divine spirit. In this sense of the word *ego*, my first task was to build a strong ego before I began the spiritual process of letting go of it.

The word *ego* has exactly the opposite meaning in most spiritual traditions. In Western Christian tradition, the word was used to indicate the prideful self that will not acknowledge any dependence on others or on the divine. In Eastern spiritual tradition, the ego usually refers to the illusion of a separate self from the absolute that stands in the way of enlightenment. Having a strong and healthy ego in the Freudian sense of the term is, I believe, essential to having a healthy and mature spiritual life. We must first possess an ego before we can freely let go of it in a healthy way.

How do I go about lessening the grip of my ego on my life in the second, spiritual sense? The first thing I had to learn to be aware of is that this process is completely out of my control and power. Trying to lessen the power of my ego is the equivalent of trying to lift myself by my own bootstraps. Only God can lessen the grip of my ego on my life by touching my heart with God's loving presence. One tiny touch of God's loving presence and I am outside my self in ecstasy and my ego is swallowed up in the glory and goodness of God. The only power my ego has in all of this is that out of my freedom to invite God in, I can ask God to come and purify me and make me worthy of the experience of God's love. Here I have to follow the path of twelve-step spirituality, acknowledge my own powerlessness, and reach out to be empowered by God: "*Let go! Let God!*"

Blondel speaks of this experience as falling into the category of those things that are simultaneously "necessary" for human fulfillment and "impossible" by human means alone. Intimate union with God is absolutely necessary for human happiness and absolutely impossible by human means alone. Therefore, if that union happens, it is because of God's power, presence, and action, and our only appropriate response is gratitude for God's merciful love. The only other power I have—and that power is also dependent on God's grace—is to live a life of compassion, always losing myself in my desire to be present in love to those in need who turn to me for help. The struggle still goes on in my spiritual life to lessen the grip my ego has on my life and be totally available to the glory of God.

An amusing anecdote may provide a clue to the nature of that struggle. In October of 1996, I returned to the Trappist Monastery, Gethsemane, for the second time. My purpose in this retreat was to seek God's grace to deepen my intimacy with God, so that I could be more effective in bringing the message of God's love to my retreatants. The retreat was in honor of the spirit of Thomas Merton. But as I drove to the monastery with a friend, I found myself speculating that many of the people who came to a Merton retreat would be aware of my work and know who I am. However, when the retreatants gathered together, it became obvious that no one there had the slightest idea who I was. So my ego became starved for recognition.

The second day of the retreat, there was a session set in the afternoon for all the retreatants to share their insights from the retreat. I thought I would have a chance to share who I was, but the entire session was given over to talking about Thomas Merton; it became obvious that all in this group were Merton "trekies." Needless to say, my ego felt deprived of due recognition. However, I returned to my private prayer, asking God to fill my heart with God's love.

On the final day of the retreat, I couldn't stand it any longer; my ego demanded a fix. After the final conference before bedtime, as we emerged from Father Matthew Kelty's talk in the chapel, some of the retreatants began to chat with each other. I selected a pleasant, friendly-looking woman and began a conversation with her. I started telling her I was a gay priest involved in a gay ministry. She immediately stopped short and asked me, "Are you one of those priests who celebrate gay marriages?"

"Yes, I am," I replied.

"Well," she said, "let's end this conversation right here!" and she stomped off in indignation. I returned to my cell, convulsed with laughter, and thanked God for not letting me get my ego fix. I spent the next couple of hours in a very peaceful God-centered rest.

I have reached the point now where I can invite God in and mean it: *Maranatha! Come, Lord Jesus! Come!* My favorite prayer at this time are the words we Catholics say after the "Our Father": "Deliver us, Lord, from all anxiety, as we wait in joyful hope for the coming of our savior, Jesus Christ." Come, Lord Jesus! Come!

I find myself daily becoming more fully identified with these words from John of the Cross's Spiritual Canticle:

> Forever at His door
> I gave my heart and soul
> my fortune, too
> I've no flock anymore,
> no other work in view
> my occupation "Love"
> it's all I do.

I intend to continue my spiritual struggle to center my life in God. Whatever time and energy I have left I will use to the best of my ability to bring the message of God's love to gays, lesbians, transsexuals, and transgendered people. I hope someday to be united with a great crowd of my gay brothers and sisters in heaven, where we will eternally celebrate God's goodness.

Epilogue

Praise to Charlie

I realize as I read through my memoirs how much I took for granted Charlie's love, presence, and support. So I want to add this epilogue to right the balance. Charlie has been at my side every step of the way since we met in Toronto, more than thirty-two years ago. He has shared my sorrows and my joys. His love has been constant and faithful. That constant love has been essential to everything that I have accomplished. He cooked the meals and kept our house clean and well organized. He drove me to every conference and workshop and sat through hundreds of sessions where he heard the same talk over and over again. He carefully edited all my publications, including this memoir. If I were perfectly truthful, this book should have been the joint memoirs of Charlie and Jack. Charlie sometimes feels identity with the older brother in the parable of the prodigal son.

Sometimes out of a deep habitual need, over so many years in the past, to keep our relationship closeted, I have not sufficiently recorded Charlie's presence and support. For example, my Sister Sheila knew and loved Charlie. He was at her bedside at our last visit, and she made him welcome. Finding it too painful to watch Sis suffer, after about a half hour, I got up to leave. But it was Charlie who reminded me of Christ's words in the Agony in the Garden of Gethsemane: "Could you not watch one hour with me!" Charlie's family has totally accepted me among them as Charlie's lover and lifemate. But my family, for the most part, with the exception of Sis, has been rather cool to him.

In January 1997, Charlie suffered a serious heart attack. I rushed back from New York City to be at his side. The doctor told Charlie he should avoid all stress and simplify his lifestyle. Charlie's close brush with death made me realize anew how much I love him and depend on him! Every day I thank God for sending him into my life. We both found it difficult to be apart three days a week, so I have discontinued my therapy practice in New York City, and we have moved back into the cabin at Starlight Lake. God willing, we hope to spend our last years together without frequent separations. During the winters, we will join our friends in Fort Lauderdale, Florida, where we have purchased a mobile home. Charlie can no longer tolerate the cold of a northern winter.

Just as, in the *Acts of the Martyrs* (quoted in John Boswell, *Same Sex Unions in Pre-Modern Europe*), Bacchus, appearing in a dream after his death, said to his gay lover, Serge: "You shall be my reward in heaven!" so it is my hope and prayer that with God's grace, after going through this life together, Charlie and I will meet beyond death and go hand in hand together into eternity.

Annotated Bibliography of the Publications of John J. McNeill

Publications concerning Sexuality and Homosexuality

"Joseph Fletcher on Sexual Behavior: A Critical Comment." *Homiletic and Pastoral Review*, Part 1, 69:7 (April 1969) and Part 2, 69:8 (May 1969).

A defense of interpersonal love as providing the necessary ethical structure for human sexuality and an attempt to define the necessary conditions of possibility for true human love to exist.

"The Christian Male Homosexual." *Homiletic and Pastoral Review*, July, August, and September 1970.

This series of three articles proposed a long overdue change in the pastoral approach to the homosexual, designed to correct social injustices and indignities suffered by homosexuals and stressing that they, too, are children of God's redemptive love in Christ.

The first article attacked stereotypes and popular misunderstandings. The second article dealt with the inadequacies of the two traditional pastoral aims in counseling homosexuals: conversion to heterosexuality or total abstinence from all sexual activity. The third article began a process of ethicomoral reevaluation, suggesting that, perhaps, within their context and under certain circumstances, homosexual relations could be objectively accepted as a lesser evil than promiscuity and thus be subjectively acceptable to those in such circumstances as morally good.

The Church and the Homosexual. Kansas City: Sheed, Andrews and McMeel, 1976.

This original publication has an *imprimi potest* from the Provincial of the New York province of the Society of Jesus. It sold vigorously through five printings. In March 1978, Pocket Books published a paperback version of the book. The first printing sold out almost immediately.

Unfortunately, Jim Andrews died shortly thereafter, and McMeel, who evidently had no liking for my book, cut off any further printing and returned a contract to me for a second book that I had signed with Jim Andrews. After one printing, the Pocket Book people also refused to issue a second printing. By the end of 1978, my book was no longer available in the United States. I waited out the requisite time and took back the copyright, and a friend, Josef Dorman, republished the book under the trademark Next Year Publications in 1985. Dorman fell ill and was unable to achieve a distribution of the Next Year Publication. In 1988 Beacon Press reissued *The Church and the Homosexual.* It has gone through five editions with a new preface in the fourth edition of 1993.

Four foreign translations of *The Church and the Homosexual* appeared: an Italian translation, *La Chiesa e l'omosessualità* (Mondadori, Rome, 1976); a Danish translation, *Kirken og den Homosexuelle* (Niels Steensens Forlag, Copenhagen, 1978); a Spanish translation, *La Iglesia ante La Homosexualidad,* volume 9 in the series Relaciones humanas y sexologia (Grijalbo, Madrid, 1979); and a French translation, *L'Église et L'Homosexuel: Un Plaidoyer* (Labor et Fides, Geneva, 1982).

In *The Church and the Homosexual,* I present three theses refuting the traditional stances taken by the Christian community regarding lesbian and gay relationships:

1. I oppose, first of all, the view that God intends all human beings to be heterosexual and that homosexuality therefore represents a deviation from God's divine plan. After years of intensive research in modern biblical scholarship, I demonstrate that there is no clear condemnation of loving homosexual relationships in scripture. Homosexual orientation has no necessary connection with sin, sickness, or failure; rather, it is a gift from God to be accepted and lived out with gratitude. Humans do not choose their orientation; they discover it as something given.

2. The second thesis is that homosexuals, rather than being a menace or threat to the values of society and the family, have special gifts and qualities and, as a part of God's creative plan, have a special contribution to make to the development of society. Indeed, if lesbians and gay men were to disappear, the further development of society toward greater humaneness would be seriously endangered.

3. In the third thesis, I argued that the love between two lesbians or gay men, assuming that it is a constructive human love, is not sinful. It can be a holy love, mediating God's presence in the human community as effectively as heterosexual love. Every human being has a God-given right to sexual love and intimacy.

Taking a Chance on God: Liberating Theology for Gays, Lesbians, and Their Lovers, Families, and Friends. Boston, Beacon Press, 1988. A paperback edition was published in 1989. A new edition with a new preface was published in 1996.

This book has been published in four foreign translations: a French translation, *Les Exclus de L'Église: Apprendre à s'Aimer* (Éditiones Filipacchi, Paris, 1993); an Italian translation, *Scommettere su Dio: Teologia della Liberazione Omosessuali* (Edizioni Sonda, Turin, 1994); a German translation, *"Sie küssten sich und weinten . . . " Homosexuelle Frauen und Männer gehen ihren spirituellen Weg* (Kosel-Verlag, Munich, 1993); and a Portugese translation, *Os excluidos da Igreja* (Circulo de Leitores, Lisbon, 1995).

Prepared by my many years of intensive study and teaching of psychodynamics at the Institutes of Religion and Health in New York City, as well as my own years of analysis, I deal with homosexuality from both spiritual and psychotherapeutic dimensions. From my years of training and experience as a psychotherapist with hundreds of gay and lesbian clients, I have combined insights from psychotherapy and spirituality to help readers overcome any interiorized homophobia, shame, guilt, and fear resulting from their religious training and from cultural and family prejudices.

Taking a Chance on God clearly distinguishes pathological religion from healthy religion, applying the principle that whatever is good theology must also be good psychology, and vice versa. This book attempts to open the door to a new ethical understanding and acceptance of homosexual relationships as morally good, and gay love as a deeper sharing in divine love. I demonstrate that those who practice pathological religion base their relationship with God on a basis of fear. Further, homophobic fundamentalist preachers demand that gays and lesbians sacrifice any hope of a life fulfilled with sexual love and intimacy to escape their fear of God's wrath. Such a service of fear would blaspheme the Christian God of love.

Freedom, Glorious Freedom: The Spiritual Journey to the Fullness of Life for Gays, Lesbians, and Everybody Else. Boston: Beacon Press 1995. The paperback was published in 1996.

There is an Italian translation: *Libertà, Gloriosa Libertà: Un cammino di spiritualità e liberazione per omosessuali credenti* (Edizioni Gruppo Abele, Turin, 1996), and recently a Portuguese translation.

The first part of the book deals with freedom of conscience and discernment of spirits. These ancient teachings of the Christian church have a special urgency for lesbian and gay people who need to free themselves from all the homophobic authorities and deal with God on a direct and personal basis.

The second part deals with the liberating process of coming out of the closet, seen as a spirit-filled effort to achieve the glory of God by becoming fully alive as gay and lesbian people.

The third part deals with twelve-step spirituality as a spiritual process of liberation from all addictions in order to experience the love of God in its fullness.

The fourth part deals with the problems that gay and lesbian persons have in becoming aware of God's special love for them and also the unique qualities present in a gay person's love for God.

In the epilogue, I attempt to express in detail a philosophical vision, looking both to the past and the future, of how gay liberation fits into the Spirit-directed evolution of human history and its role in the ongoing struggle for human liberation.

"Homosexuality, Lesbianism, and the Future: The Creative Role of the Gay Community in Building a More Humane Society." In *A Challenge to*

Love: Gay and Lesbian Catholics in the Church. Edited by Robert Nugent. New York: Crossroad, 1983.

I argue that the emergence of a visible gay community at this time in human history is providential because gay people have special gifts to give that the whole human society stands in need of.

"Homosexuality: Challenging the Church to Grow." *The Christian Century*, March 11, 1987.

This article presents the argument that gays, who were excluded from the Old Testament community based on a procreative covenant, are explicitly included by the Holy Spirit in Acts 8.

"The Gay Response to AIDS." *The Way: A Review of Contemporary Spirituality* 28:4 (October 1988).

An argument for the special need of gay people with AIDS to find a resurrection-based spirituality.

"Homosexuality." In *The New Dictionary of Catholic Spirituality*. Edited by Michael Downey. Collegeville, Minn.: Liturgical Press, 1993.

An attempt to locate the uniqueness of gay and lesbian spirituality.

"Spiritual Values in Therapy: A Theological Perspective." *The Bulletin of the National Guild of Catholic Psychiatrists*, vol. 26 (1980).

"Tapping Deeper Roots: Integrating the Spiritual Dimension into Professional Practice with Lesbian and Gay Clients." *The Journal of Pastoral Care* 48:4 (1994).

Presents the argument that gays are in special need of dealing with their spirituality in therapy in order to learn to distinguish pathological elements from healthy spirituality.

Books and Articles dealing with Blondel's Philosophy of Action

The Blondelian Synthesis: A Study of the Influence of German Philosophical Sources on Blondel's Method and Thought. Volume 1 in the series Studies in the History of Christian Thought. Edited by Heiko Oberman. Leiden: E.J. Brill, 1966.

In a separate appendix in *Freedom, Glorious Freedom*, I explain the influence of Blondel's understanding of freedom on my writings concerning homosexuality.

"Freedom of Conscience in Theological Perspective." In *Conscience: Its Freedom and Limitations*. Edited by William C. Bier. New York: Fordham University Press, 1971.

In several articles presented to professional philosophical organizations, I spelled out the meaning of freedom in Blondel's thought.

"Necessary Structures of Freedom." *Proceedings of the Jesuit Philosophical Association*, 1968.

"The Relation between Philosophy and Religion in Blondel's Thought." *Proceedings of the American Catholic Philosophical Association*, 1969.

"Freedom and the Future." *Theological Studies*, September 1972.
Applied Blondel's thought to issues in genetics.

"Blondel on the Subjectivity of Moral Decision Making." *Proceedings of the American Catholic Philosophical Association*, 1974.
Presents the argument that all moral decision making has as its ultimate dimension a discernment that the individual's will is in conformity with the divine will of the Spirit dwelling within the self.

"Martin Buber's Biblical Philosophy of History." *International Philosophical Quarterly* 6 (March 1966).
Presents the argument that there are unique moments in history because there is a real existential dialogue between individuals and God.